# 30 DAYS

to

# FINANCIAL EXCELLENCE

Learn to Master Your Money

Like a Personal Finance Pro

**INGE NATALIE HOL**

30 DAYS TO FINANCIAL EXCELLENCE
Learn to Master Your Money Like a Personal Finance Pro
Copyright © 2020 Inge Natalie Hol

100 Steps Publishing
Inge@100stepstoFI.com
IngeNatalieHol.com

Cover and interior design by Domini Dragoone - dominidragoone.com
Editorial services provided by Noel Editorial - noeleditorial.com
Cover images: JaneKelly/iStock, Salamatik/iStock

ISBN (print): 978-84-09-21525-6
ISBN (ebook): 978-84-09-21715-1
ISBN (audiobook): 9781664942714

**Disclaimer**

*30 Days to Financial Excellence* is intended to help others on their way to better money management. The information presented is for informational purposes only and is solely the expression of the author's opinion. The author is not offering any legal, investing, or tax advice and is not liable for any actions prompted or caused by the information in this book. While every attempt has been made to verify any information presented in this book, the author is not responsible for any errors, inaccuracies, or omissions. Consult a professional if you have any concerns or doubts regarding your specific personal situation. No liability is assumed for losses or damages due to the information provided.

To my parents, May and Els, I couldn't have been luckier. Thank you for being the best parents I could wish for, for all your love, and for everything I am thanks to you both.

# Get your free workbook

**Get your free workbook to accompany *30 Days to Financial Excellence*, along with other exclusive materials.**

Helping my readers make a difference in their financial lives is the thing I enjoy the most about writing my books. To help you get the most out of this book, I've put together a free workbook for you. Download these fifteen pages of exclusive content and start building your new financial life today.

By signing up for my newsletter, you'll instantly get all the following free materials:

★ The accompanying *30 Days to Financial Excellence* Workbook

★ Access to my online course, *The Secrets of the 7 Income Streams*

★ A sample of my *100 Steps to Financial Independence* book

I occasionally send newsletters with practical tips, interesting news, new book releases, and pre-release specials.

You can get the workbook, online course, and sample for free at:

IngeNatalieHol.com/30daysdownload

# Contents

# INTRODUCTION

## MY SEARCH FOR HAPPINESS

One Sunday morning, as I was sitting on the beach at sunrise, I watched my two big Labrador rescues running along the water, trying to outrun each other. My little terrier rescue, not interested in playing with the other two, sat peacefully next to me, her eyes closed, face turned toward the upcoming sun, ears gently flapping in the breeze. In that moment, it struck me how easy it can be to enjoy life. To experience intense pleasure with so little: the wide-open space of the beach, the light of the early morning, the wind stroking your face and playing with your ears, the seawater splashing up and tickling your belly as you race your best friend . . .

I hadn't planned to sit down on the beach. After all, as it was a Sunday, there was more than enough I had to get done, both at home and in preparation for work the following week. So I was impatient for my dogs to get their run over with and head back home. But dogs are the ultimate happiness teachers, showing how beautiful things can be without the cares, problems, stress, or sadness we humans might experience in daily life. So when I saw them thoroughly enjoying what I had planned as a short detour to the beach, so content in that moment, I just had to sit down and be present with them too.

Taking it all in, it hit me how challenging it can be to be happy with the simple things and experiences I have. Of course, we're all busy with life. Like many, I feel I hardly have time to run a household, go to work, look after children (or pets, in my case), and see friends and family, let alone find time to spend on myself and tackle fears and worries that keep me up at night.

So that Sunday morning on the beach, when my dogs showed me how beautiful life is and how easy it can be to enjoy, I made a promise to myself to figure out how I could create a lifestyle that allowed me to experience more happiness, fulfillment, and joy every day. I didn't want to overhaul my life and live a completely different version of it. I just needed to make some small changes, but with a big enough impact.

The next few days, I kept reminding myself of this promise, and the more I thought about how to be happier, the more I realized my habits—and in particular my financial habits—were at the core of the problem. From there it was a small jump to work out that that's also where most of the solutions lay. It was in the days following that trip to the beach that I decided that I was going to make it a priority to live up to the name a colleague once gave me—"Inge Ninja"—and become not a martial artist, but a personal finance and happiness ninja.

Over the next few months, I was determined to make the changes I needed to make to kickstart my new financial life and increase my happiness. I spent hours and hours researching, analyzing, and planning what I needed to do. And little by little I mapped out a plan.

I knew one of the key things I wanted was to finally go on holiday that year, so I set up a savings fund to which my husband and I both started contributing each month. I also wanted to spend a little less time in the office and more at home, so I decided to take a small pay cut and get somebody in to cover me a few hours a week. Last, I felt a desire to tap into my creativity and start a side hustle to turn into another income stream, so I used some of that time I now had at home to start realizing this dream.

Along with adding in more moments of happiness, I also needed to address some fears I felt I had put off dealing with but that kept creeping up on me at times. A lot of those worries were again related to our financial situation. They not only made me feel nervous but—more importantly—the fear stopped me from taking action. Sometimes it is easier to just keep going than to address worries head-on. It's like when you have a toothache, but you hold off going to the dentist because you're too scared of what he or she might tell you. Needless to say, the longer you wait, the worse it will be. And it's the same with managing your money.

It felt uncomfortable that I was still paying back my student loan more than fifteen years after graduating. It gave me the unpleasant sensation that my past was controlling my present. So I put together a strategy to become debt-free. I also wanted to get rid of the fear of not knowing whether we'd ever have enough money to retire, so I made sure my husband and I finally set up a retirement fund and started contributing to it. I furthermore found ways to increase my monthly contribution to my savings account and started building up a financial security net in case we ever needed to fall back on some money if our income fell away.

It took a long time to find the solutions and implement them. But the changes in how I felt were incredible. Just starting some of these new habits, even if I was still a long time away from paying off my loan or saving enough money for it to be able to support us if that was needed, made me so much less afraid of what the future would hold. For the first time in a very long time, I felt that *I* was in control of what was happening instead of life just happening to me. Every time I logged in to my bank accounts, I saw my goals slowly becoming reality as my holiday fund started to fill up, as I was saving an emergency fund, and as my debt was finally going down faster than ever before. As I started my side hustle, spending that little extra bit of time on it and the small additional income each week made me feel much happier. And although my retirement was still about thirty years away, I felt reassured setting aside money toward it now. This all seemed to take a big burden off me and give me a much brighter outlook on life.

With all the responsibilities we have each day to work, look after our families, pay bills, and live up to social obligations, it can be really hard to take a moment and pursue the life we intended to live. Whether that's big-scale traveling the world or simply stopping to appreciate happy moments in our daily lives, it's not until we take a step back and force ourselves to take control that we can really start to become what we want to be.

I have discovered that by changing our mindset, implementing new habits, and mastering some essential financial knowledge, anybody can experience not just a more secure financial life, but also an increased feeling of happiness.

In the end, I found it wasn't that difficult to make these changes. But it can be challenging if you don't know where to start. That's why I wrote this book. I want you to experience the same outcome I still feel every day: less stress and worries and more happiness and empowerment. But I want you to get there without needing to invest all the time and energy I spent figuring this out. I've tried to make this as easy as possible for you.

In this book I've laid out the exact path you can take to become a personal finance ninja too. In as little as 30 days, I will show you exactly what you can do to achieve this. Written as a practical guide, this book allows you to instantly turn around your finances and build a healthy and happy financial life, for now and for your future. It will take you from where you are now down the path to a new financial life, one day and one step at a time.

During the next 30 days, we'll cover the eight essential elements that make up your personal finances. Each day will focus on just one aspect of your finances and end with a clear, practical action plan and a few steps to get that part of your finances on track. Starting today, I will guide you through the process of digging up, dusting off, sorting, and straightening, and then planning, working, and molding your finances into what you *want* them to be.

I am confident you'll soon look back and wonder why you took so long to start taking action.

This isn't a state you'll reach overnight, though; it requires work and dedication. And unfortunately, the longer you've ignored your personal finance issues, the longer it will take you to get back on track and resolve this once and for all. But you can do this! All you need is to trust yourself and the program, some time over the next 30 days (or more if you decide to go at a slower pace), and the willpower to start a new episode in your personal financial life.

This book is, of course, about your finances, but it is only a means to an end. The reason for looking at your finances isn't simply to become better at managing your money. The bigger, much more exciting reason to dig into this topic and set up a system you can proactively operate is to make your dreams, whether long term or day to day, come true—just as my journey didn't start with money, but with a longing to pursue more happiness. Wishing and dreaming is one thing, but they are only dreams until you start to act on them concretely.

## How to Use This Book

I wanted this book to be practical for you, so I've kept each chapter short and to the point. There are no long explanations or theories about personal finance and financial management, just the key information you need to know followed by the practical steps you can implement instantly to get that particular area of your finances organized once and for all. My idea is that you can read each chapter in just a few minutes and get started implementing that day's assignments as soon as possible.

The book is divided into 30 days and can be completed in one month. But if you can't commit to working on your finances every day for one month straight, then that's okay too. Find a structure and timeline that work for you. That could be working on it two or three times a week or completing several tasks over the weekend. Any schedule is totally fine; what's important is that it works for *you*. Work on the assignments regularly. You'll gain momentum and keep up your motivation as you see small improvements linking together and propelling you toward a wealthier and happier life.

## How is this book set up?

There are eight parts in this book, each part corresponding to one major area of your finances. All except the first part are subdivided into four topics, and these topics will usually correspond to the following format.

★ **Analyze your current situation:** Usually the first task in each part, you'll map out what your current situation looks like. In order to know where to go, the first thing you need to do is find out where you are now.

★ **Implement a new habit:** You'll learn the single most important habit you can put into action to make a difference in each of the eight areas of your finances.

★ **Plan where to go:** You'll set realistic targets for each area and plan how to get there.

★ **Pro tip:** At the end of most sections, you'll find a more advanced habit to adopt with the focus on making a lasting long-term change.

## 10 tips to get the most out of the next 30 days

Before we dive into the real content of this book, here are ten quick and easy tips to help you get the most out of this 30-day program:

1.  Know that everybody's journey is different. Don't judge, don't feel judged, don't try to be like others. Follow your own path. Yes, your neighbor might earn more money, have inherited from her parents, drive a bigger car, or have better retirement funds offered by her employer . . . Well, tough luck for you, but there's nothing you can do about that. Focus on what you *can* do something about, and that is your *own* financial life. There's no point dwelling on "what ifs," as that isn't getting you closer to achieving financial excellence.

2.  Set aside time each day to work on your finances. Mark this time in your calendar. If you can't arrange for a set time every day, look ahead and identify your timetable. If you are short of time or fear you need a lot of time for each task based on the state of your finances, complete one task a week. This means you still get it all done in just over six months. Just make sure to schedule your time. Don't leave it up to chance; plan for your financial success to happen.

3.  Don't move on to the next task until you are done with the previous one. Most action plans build on the previous ones, so there's not much point jumping ahead if you've missed a step.

4.  Get a notebook to take notes when you go through each day's activity. Write down thoughts, plans, and the day's exercises. Alternatively, create a digital file if you prefer to work from your computer.

5.  Find an accountability partner who is willing to check in on your progress to keep you on track. Better still, find somebody who is

happy to join you on this challenge and go through it together. By sharing your goals, you instantly increase the likelihood of achieving success. Post regular updates on social media using #30DaystoFinancialExcellence to allow others to see your progress and maybe get inspired by you.

6. Take action. You can spend hours, days, and sometimes even weeks finding the perfect solution for something, but as the saying goes, "Imperfect action is better than perfect inaction." Don't overthink, get started.

7. Get your partner, children, or housemates on board, but don't expect them to be as motivated as you. This is your project; you started this, so see yourself as the principal engine behind improving your finances. If they start sharing that motivation; great, if not, then at least make sure they know what you're doing and why it is important to you.

8. Remember that financial excellence is not something most people busy themselves with. You'll be doing things that friends, family, and colleagues might have never thought about. They might even tell you not to worry so much or that you've become frugal or obsessive. If that bothers you, then ask yourself how much they excel at their own personal finances. If they don't and live a fairly average life that includes financial worries and an uncertain future (if you don't know, then ask yourself how they are financing all the things they own and do), then remember you're doing this because you want a better financial situation for you and your family. Ignore their opinions and just get on with this book. If they do seem proficient at personal finance management, then by all means go and talk to them about how they achieved their successes—and learn from them.

9. With everything you do, always ask yourself what would make you truly happy. When you set goals, don't forget about your and your family's happiness. It's not more important to have money than it is to be healthy and happy. What does money mean to you, and what does it let you do? Having $1,000,000 in a bank account isn't much

of a goal if you don't know why you're pursuing this. Money itself shouldn't be a goal. Your goal should be what you want to do with your money: travel the world, buy a second house by the lake, work a job you love even if it doesn't pay amazingly, be able to spend time with your family, volunteer . . . Don't aim for a million if it means working sixty-hour weeks for the rest of your life at the expense of what you truly love.

10. Be aware of excuses you might use to avoid completing the tasks, such as feeling the work is difficult or boring. Be that as it may, you'll need to get through it. And what are 30 days in your life if it means you will save money, take away worries, and live a happier and richer life?

# PART ONE

# YOUR MONEY MINDSET

Your mindset is the collection of beliefs and assumptions about yourself and, in particular, about your skills, intelligence, and abilities. It determines how you deal with challenges, experience learning, and define and achieve success.

Psychologist Carol Dweck believes that there are two types of mindsets: a fixed mindset and a growth mindset. People with a fixed mindset believe our traits, intelligence, and abilities are an innate constellation that is set for the rest of our lives. People with a growth mindset, on the other hand, believe our skills and intelligence are flexible and can be learned or developed throughout our lives.

People with a fixed mindset are more likely to believe they can't do anything about a problem and give up trying to change their situation, while those with a growth mindset are more likely to tackle problems actively, find new solutions, and learn new skills when needed.

As your mindset plays an important role in your abilities to tackle any challenge in life, including those presented by your financial life, you're going to start your 30-day journey to financial excellence with a closer look at your thoughts and beliefs about your money management skills. Then, by adopting and using the growth mindset, you'll transform any negative thoughts into positive and empowering beliefs so that you'll be all set to truly achieve financial excellence.

# Day 1

## WHAT'S YOUR MONEY MINDSET?

The way you think about money is at the base of your financial habits, decisions, and actions. While you might not always be aware of them, your feelings and thoughts have a huge impact on your ability to live a satisfying financial life. Without the attitude, motivation, and belief that you can achieve something, it's difficult to do so. How likely do you think it is that you can live a financially successful life if deep down you believe you are a complete failure when it comes to managing your money, or if you believe that money is just not important?

So let's start by finding out how you really feel about money. Once you've gained a picture of some of these beliefs, you can start working on turning them into empowering affirmations.

Look at the statements below and mark each with a 1 (agree), 2 (neutral), or 3 (disagree). Remember, you are doing this exercise just for you, so be honest with yourself.

- [ ] I've never been good with money.

- [ ] Wanting more money is a sign of greed.

- [ ] My parents/partner/teachers told me that as a woman/man/ when I was a child/because of my high-paying job/because of my low-paying job/etc., I didn't need to worry about money.

☐ I never have enough money for my personal goals.

☐ I've never prioritized money.

☐ I'm always broke.

☐ I find it hard to make (more) money.

☐ I'm always drowning in debt.

☐ I will never be rich.

☐ There are lots of reasons I don't have money.

☐ Even if I work really hard, I'll never get paid enough money.

☐ Rich people are rich only because they were either lucky or greedy.

☐ Thinking about my money makes me feel stressed, exhausted, fearful, or worried.

☐ Money is at the root of a lot of evil.

☐ Choosing wealth means giving up happiness.

When you've gone through them all, total your points for these statements. Read on to find out what your score says about your attitude toward money.

**15-25: Need help.** You don't feel very confident or optimistic about your ability to manage your money, and you fear you might never feel that way. You're concerned this will affect you and your family long term, and you don't know where to start to get out of this situation and turn things around once and for all.

**26-35: Getting there.** You don't feel totally hopeless about your money skills, but you wonder whether you might be heading in the wrong direction. You recognize the need to get your financial life organized, and you'd like to feel more confident about your financial situation and future.

**36-45: Pretty savvy.** You seem confident about your money management skills and feel excited about perfecting your ability to have an exceptional financial life. You know there is much to do still, but that doesn't make you feel desperate about the situation. You're motivated to tackle your finances and to move on to the next level of being money savvy.

Regardless of which category you scored in, over the next four weeks this book will give you the skills you need to build a stable and secure financial life now as well as for your future!

## *Day 1* ACTION PLAN
# Contemplate your financial beliefs.

1. Of the statements you marked above, note which three seem to be the most true or the most surprising, revealing, or shocking to you.

2. Answer the following questions in your notebook: Why do you think you have these thoughts or feelings in particular? Is it because of your upbringing, your past or current environment, or something that you've experienced?

# Day 2

## CREATE NEW MONEY BELIEFS

There is a famous adage that says, "What you think you become." It suggests that the thoughts we allow to exist in our minds can help us on our journey to improvement and progress. Similarly, negative thoughts can be obstacles that can keep us from moving forward.

On day 1, you identified limiting beliefs that might stop you from realizing your true potential when it comes to personal finance management. If you keep telling yourself that you don't have enough money or can't be financially responsible, one way or another this will become your truth.

Today, I want you to transform those statements into a more positive outlook. From this point on, you need to trust that you—and your beliefs and your reality—can change.

Switching a negative belief into a positive one isn't simple, so let's take small steps by rewriting the statements a little at a time, until after 5-8 steps you've created a positive affirmation. Moving through the sequence from negative to positive belief becomes a lot easier in this way, as you can see here:

*I've never been good with money* **can become:**
I've not yet been good with money.
I can learn to be good with money.
I want to and will be good with money.

I have started learning about how to be better with money.
I am starting to get better with money.
I am good with money.
I am great with money.

**I'm always drowning in debt can become:**
I'm always drowning in debt—but that will change starting today.
I'm always drowning in debt, but I am taking action.
I'm always drowning in debt, but I've already started paying things off.
I used to drown in debt, but I have paid off one debt completely.
I used to drown in debt, but I am now on my way to a debt-free life.
I used to drown in debt, but I am now debt-free.

These statement transformations are personal, and you can decide where to take each one. There is no one correct positive progression for each statement. As everybody's journey is different, the process of rewriting the statements is a very personal experience.

As you move from negative to more positive, your aim is to find the tipping point: the place just beyond your current level of comfort. That statement will be the one to turn into your new truth or affirmation.

## *Day 2* ACTION PLAN
# Align your thoughts with your goals.

1. Take the three statements you identified as most accurate or impactful on day 1 and rewrite them into a positive statement by making gradual changes until you have a set of gradually transforming affirmations for each of the three original ones.

2. As you read and move through the transformation from negative to more positive statements, determine which new rewritten description you feel most comfortable with and can identify with. Then, take the next level up toward the positive end. Those will become your affirmations to work on.

3. Take your three new statements and put them on the bathroom mirror, on your fridge, or in your diary. Read them out loud every morning and evening, meditate on them, or journal about them. With time they'll become your new truths. Let your mind guide you, and you'll soon find that you start to adapt your behavior to these new truths.

4. When your new statements are no longer uncomfortable and start to become your new reality, move on to the next level. You should replace each one as soon as you identify with the statement and no longer see it as a challenge to believe in.

# YOUR EXPENSES

Your expenses play a key role in this 30-day course. Together with your income, they form the principal elements of your finances. If you spend more than you earn, you build up debt, which means you are jeopardizing your financial situation with the negatives that debt brings, such as interest payments and a lower credit score. If you earn more than you spend, on the other hand, you are investing in a secure financial future by building up savings.

If you aren't in charge of your expenses, you will find that your expenses are in charge of you. That might sound dramatic, but spending money is now easier than ever, as we have a twenty-four-hour connection to millions of online shopping options, while self-control and planning often are not things we're good at when it comes to money, especially in times of stress.

By not taking full control of your expenses, you give your expenses free rein, which can result in a buildup of debts or a lack of money put toward your financial future. If you feel you never have any money left, then let's get started actively managing every dollar, euro, pound, or whatever currency you get paid in. Start seeing your dollars as a team that you need to direct and instruct. Make your money team follow a path where everybody knows what they are doing and how they contribute to the bigger picture, and strike a balance between enjoyment of life as it is now and investment in a secure future.

My aim in this section of these 30 days is not for you to cut your expenses down to the absolute minimum, save aggressively, and start thinking of expenses as bad. On the contrary, expenses allow you to provide for yourself and your family and to have fun. Expenses are, in many ways, a good thing.

What I want you to do is make sure your expenses are within your means and that they align with your overall financial objectives and happiness. It can be easy and tempting to spend money on things because you've always done so. Therefore, in this part, I want you to look at your expenses more critically and determine whether they coordinate with what you really *want* to spend your money on.

# Day 3

## TRACK YOUR EXPENSES

Our principal focus in this section is to streamline your expenses with your income and objectives so you can start to shave off some costs and put that money toward other personal finance goals, such as paying off debt, building up savings, and investing in your retirement.

To get started, you'll need to find out more about your current expense patterns: Where does your money go each month? What percentage of your expenses is dedicated to groceries, dining out, savings, or car expenses? Without knowing what you spend your money on, it'll be difficult to make structural changes and work toward improving your financial situation.

This means you're going to need to keep a detailed record of your expenses. Whether you do this down to the very last cent or use estimated or rounded numbers is up to you; what's important is that you do it in a way that allows you to keep up this new habit for at least a month. A full month's worth of data will give you valuable insight into what you typically spend your money on. It allows you to make well-founded decisions as to where you can cut expenses, which will help you during the remainder of these 30 days when you start planning your other financial areas.

You can keep track of your money in a variety of ways: in a notebook, on a spreadsheet, or with one of the many apps such as Mint or YNAB you can install on your phone. The choice is yours, but don't spend too much time investigating the various options instead of actually getting started.

If you've never tracked your money before, this new habit might take you a little while to get into. Try to keep at it, even if you forget to do so one day. If you skip a day or two, it's not the end of the world. Fill in what you remember and pick it up again and continue onward. It's okay if it isn't absolutely perfect!

## *Day 3* ACTION PLAN
## Follow your money.

1. Get a notebook, open a spreadsheet, or investigate some of the mobile apps available and decide how you are going to register your expenses. Remember, you can always change later on, so make sure to get started today and don't go through a lengthy decision-making process. Consider ease of use as well as the portability of the system, though, if you want to update your register whenever and wherever you are.

2. Always register your expenses at a set time: every evening, as soon as you purchase something, or right at the start of your lunch break.

3. Check daily for any expenses that come out of your bank accounts as automatic payments you have authorized (utilities, mortgage, etc.).

4. Create logical categories in your expenses register once you have a bit more data to add some structure. Housing costs (mortgage/rent, water, gas, electricity, taxes), car expenses (fuel, insurance, maintenance), and fun money (meals out, date nights, and family trips) are examples of umbrella categories that can help create organization for their subcategories.

5. Get at least one month's worth of data, more if you can. You don't need to hold off continuing with the rest of this book, though; just keep registering as you go along. Once you've got a full month, you can always revisit some of the tasks in this book.

6. Try and make this a habit to keep up forever. Once you get going it will become easier, and the advantage of knowing what and how you spend over long periods of time is that it will help you make even better financial decisions in the future.

# Day 4

## CUT DOWN AN EXPENSE

To take matters into your own hands and start building the foundation of a brighter and more secure financial future, today you are going to identify where you can save money by spending (a little) less. The money you'll be saving will come in handy in myriad ways, as you'll discover in more detail in later days of this 30-day plan.

Once you manage to spend less than you earn, you can use what is left over from your income to build savings, investment, and retirement funds. The bigger the gap between what you earn and what you spend, the more you can invest in your financial security network and future.

While I don't want you to rigorously start cutting out all the fun and become a nonspender in a single day, I am also sure there are areas you can identify that are easy to save some money in and involve less of a lifestyle change. Here are some ideas:

★ Pack your lunches or bring your coffee to work instead of buying these every day.

★ Give up smoking.

★ Use public transportation, cycle, or walk instead of taking the car.

★ Set a limit on the amount of money you spend on dinners or drinks out with friends.

- ★ Look for cheaper brands when grocery shopping and pay special attention to any offers or promotions on products.

- ★ Cut out subscriptions or memberships you haven't been using recently, such as a gym membership, cable TV, or magazine subscriptions.

- ★ For those monthly payments you can't cut out altogether, find cheaper alternatives. Can you go for a cheaper mobile phone plan, or is there an electricity company that offers better rates?

- ★ Identify ways to make small behavioral changes to save on your electricity or water bills: turn off lights and disconnect appliances when you're not there, turn off the water when brushing your teeth, or have a one-minute-shorter shower.

Be creative when you look at your expenses. I am sure you can come up with more ideas to save on some of them.

## *Day 4* ACTION PLAN
# Shave one expense.

1. Think about which expense you might want to limit. Start with just one. Cutting out too much at a time might take away all your motivation if it requires a lot of sacrifice or change.

2. Estimate how much you think you'd be able to save with moderate efforts. Be realistic, but set yourself a big enough challenge for it to be useful and exciting.

3. Start saving, and at the end of each day, week, or month, make sure to set aside the amount you estimate you have saved during that period. This can be either by taking the cash you have saved out of your wallet and putting it in a glass jar or by transferring the money into a separate bank account. By laying the money aside, you'll appreciate how you've already achieved much more than if you let it continue to live in your wallet or regular bank account.

4. Later on during these 30 days, you'll find ways to put this money to good use, such as by setting up an emergency fund, paying off debt, or saving up for a long-term goal.

# Day 5

## CREATE A SPENDING PLAN

The ultimate way to power up your journey to financial excellence is by proactively taking control over the money you spend. That means before you receive any money from your monthly paycheck or another income source, first determine how you'll want to spend your money. Do this by setting up a spending plan: a blueprint that helps you make decisions as to where your money should go, instead of waiting until the end of the month to find out where your money has gone.

A spending plan's principal goal is to help you plan out how much you want to spend on each of your various expense categories. It also helps you ensure you don't spend more money than comes in each month—fairly important if you don't want to go into debt (further). Last, it allows you to set aside money for long-term goals, such as savings, paying down debt, or retirement contributions. These types of payments are often forgotten without a plan. Don't leave it until you've spent most of your money to decide how much you might have left over to assign to long-term goals. Use a spending plan to help you actively *plan* for how much to save each month.

As you start keeping track of where your money is going (as we saw in day 3), it should slowly become clear roughly how much you spend on each category. Use that to set up a first-draft plan. If you spend an average of $100 on your weekly trip to the supermarket, then put $400 or $450 down in your spending plan for groceries so you know you'll be needing that amount each month for your grocery shopping. Follow a similar strategy to fill in the other parts of your spending until you have a "closed budget," meaning you know what you'll be spending every dollar of your paycheck on.

Your first plan will probably not involve a great deal of planning on how you *want* to spend your money, but rather mainly reflect how you are *currently* spending your money. That's absolutely fine, and, in fact, it's the best place to start. You can start making small adjustments each month from here on. Once you become more accustomed to creating, updating, and following a spending plan, you'll be pleased to see how much this will help you when it gets to long-term financial planning.

## *Day 5* ACTION PLAN
## Create your first-draft spending plan.

Using bank statements, receipts, and your estimating abilities, create a first draft of a spending plan:

1. List your expense categories and subcategories.

2. Calculate or estimate the total you expect to spend monthly for each category.

3. Don't forget to identify categories that are not recurrent each month, such as presents, your trip to the hairdresser's, and car maintenance costs. These expenses might not come out of your accounts each month, but they should still be part of your plan. The best way to account for these irregular expenses is to think of how much you pay for these and divide that by the number of months there are in between each expense. For example, if you pay $60 to go to the hairdresser every three months, put down $20 per month in your plan for this expense.

4. During the rest of this month, consult your plan daily and update your expenses so you always know how much you have already spent in each category and how much you still have left until the end of the month.

5. Update your plan as you go if you realize you need more money for a category by taking it from another category that needs less than you estimated.

6. At the start of each month, set a new spending plan for that month. Adjust your spending amounts per category based on specifics coming up that month (think: birthdays, trips away, etc.) as well as your deeper understanding of your spending in general.

# Day 6

## SET A SPENDING PLAN GOAL

Your spending plan makes your current financial spending a lot more visible. And while you've already started adjusting your spending a little by limiting one expense (day 4), I expect you have other expenses you feel are too heavily budgeted for. This could be anything from your Internet subscription to your car insurance or the amount you spend on new clothes.

So the next step on this journey is to set targets for your spending patterns, and plan how to adjust them little by little to what you want them to be. That paves the way to a target plan to work toward over the next several months, so that your spending becomes even more conscious and in line with what you want to spend on, while at the same time it clears up more money to improve your financial future.

The easiest way to get started with creating a target spending plan is to use the 50/20/30 rule as your guideline. According to this rule, you should aim to spend 50% of your money on direct, essential living expenses (rent/mortgage, groceries, utilities, car expenses, etc.), 20% on savings (investments, savings accounts, retirement accounts, paying down debt, etc.), and 30% on fun or discretionary expenses (date nights, holidays, those new shoes just because you love them).

Bear in mind that this rule is just a guideline, however, and in no way does it fit everybody. You might need to spend substantially more on your living expenses for whatever reason; the 20% savings might be unattainable at the moment, or maybe it actually sounds too conservative to you. The real challenge is to find the percentages that seem right to you—and note that they are likely to change again in the future as your lifestyle and expenses evolve.

## *Day 6* ACTION PLAN
## Assess your expenses with the 50/20/30 rule.

1. Pull out the spending plan you put together on day 5 and calculate the percentages of your expense categories. What is your current distribution of funds for your essential, savings, and discretionary expenses?

2. Determine how far off you are from the 50/20/30 guideline.

3. Decide what would be a reasonable distribution to aim for. Adapt the 50/20/30 numbers as you see fit, but remember that when you add them up, they have to equal 100 to represent 100% of your expenses.

4. Taking your ideal version of the 50/20/30 distribution, see how far you are from that at the moment. Which small adjustments would you be able to make in the future to slowly start shifting toward a more desired distribution of your expenses? Say you'd like to get to a 18% savings expenses percentage but are currently at 10%. What small steps can you take now or in the near future to, little by little, move closer to 18%? Brainstorm some ideas; we'll start implementing some of these on day 8.

PART THREE

# YOUR SAVINGS

Your savings are for your short-term needs, your long-term dreams, and anything in between. Having savings for short-term necessities such as your taxes, a computer replacement, or all of this year's Christmas presents can be hugely reassuring and take away financial worries. Building up savings for long-term goals can be exciting and motivating, whether that's for a down payment for your house, a holiday to Paris, a new gadget you've had your eyes on for a long time, or your stress-free retirement.

Growing your savings means you are investing in your future. What you save for tomorrow you can't spend today, so it requires self-control and a plan. The more you save, the more you build toward a future that you can shape. Of course, nobody knows what the future holds, and living just for the future can take away the joy of today. But the opposite—living in the present, not planning for your future, and leaving your financial security up to others, luck, or chance—is a hard gamble, one you will regret when the future is just around the corner and turns out not to be very secure or abundant.

A life without savings means you don't allow yourself to dream and work toward something. As a consequence, for any big purchase you'll need to take out a loan, which makes purchases much more expensive due to the interest you will pay. It means no anticipation or feelings of satisfaction in working toward something and having controlled the impulse to buy now on credit. No or little savings also portends you will likely be unable to retire at your desired age because you won't have the funds to pay for your needs once you stop receiving an income.

No savings means no security net. And that security net is dramatically important to have if you want to avoid the risk of losing even the daily essentials in your life. No security net signifies you might not be able to repair your washing machine when it suddenly breaks down. It means that if you lose your job, you might need to cancel that holiday your children have been looking forward to all year. It can mean the loss of health, mobility, or even life itself if you can't pay for an emergency medical treatment.

**Now, here is what life with savings looks like:**

★ Peace of mind knowing you can deal with unexpected emergencies, thanks to your well-funded emergency fund

★ A sense of satisfaction as you are working toward a car fund so when you need to replace your car, you can pay for it in cash instead of having to finance it with an expensive loan

★ A feeling of excitement as you are working toward important goals in life and you know that each month brings you a little bit closer to each one

★ The knowledge that you will be able to retire comfortably, thanks to the contributions you are making to your retirement funds

Whether you're saving $500, $20, or $1 a month isn't the principal worry at this point. Progress is progress, and even if you don't believe there is any advantage in setting $1 a month aside toward a big goal, trust me: there is. It might look small today, but once you start, you'll find there will be lots of ways to speed up this process—whether that's extra money left over at the end of the month, a tax refund, or a work bonus. Once you begin, you'll find other ways to contribute to your savings. But if you don't start, you won't have a dedicated savings account to put your tax refund or bonus, apart from in your wallet to spend at the next opportunity.

Having savings brings much more than some spare money in a bank account; it gives you a lifestyle and emotional satisfaction that is beyond compare.

# Day 7

## SET YOUR SAVINGS GOALS

There's never much satisfaction in doing anything if you don't know why you're doing it. I believe this is particularly true for your savings: if you don't know what you're saving for, it isn't nearly as much fun or exciting as when you have a specific goal (or several goals) in mind. When you can picture that goal clearly, knowing with every contribution you're one step closer to that objective, that's when the excitement and dedication really kick in.

So what are some of the goals you want to save up for? A helpful way to map out ideas is to think of short-term (less than 2 years), mid-term (2–5 years), and long-term (more than 5 years) targets. Anything you want or think you might need to buy in those time frames that is outside of your regular monthly or yearly expenses counts. This can be next summer's holiday, a new phone, a new (secondhand) car, a house, your wedding, a new jacket, refurbishing your kitchen, a spa treatment for yourself, your child's university fees, or an early retirement.

The key to reaching your savings goals isn't earning big money and then making big contributions. It's about small and consistent steps that will get you to your goals gradually, with time and persistence. Some goals might be more important to you, others might be more urgent, and some might be faraway goals that you have a lot of time left to reach.

When it comes to planning your savings targets, don't sacrifice your long-term dreams for your more immediate ones. One day you'll wake up to find that the future is here and that you never got around to saving for that trip around the world you wanted to make upon retiring. Set up a savings account for your faraway dreams too. Commit to making monthly payments toward each and every goal. Find ways to cut expenses and free up or bring in some extra money to get your savings kick-started.

You don't have to make equal contributions toward all your goals. If you set aside $50 a month to save up for your next vacation and another $50 for a new washing machine, you could probably also set aside $5 for your dream cottage by the lake for when you retire. A small step, and an amount that might seem insignificant, but it gets you started and prevents you from forgetting about that dream you have. And of course, whatever you save this month might well be doubled next month.

## *Day* 7 **ACTION PLAN**
# Name your dreams and start saving for them.

1. Note any of your savings goals or dreams that come to mind.

2. Divide your goals into short-term (less than 2 years), mid-term (2–5 years), and long-term (more than 5 years) goals. Prioritize them as best you can, not by deadline, but by how important they are to you.

3. Estimate how much you need for each goal, when you'd need the money by, and how much you need to set aside monthly to reach that goal by the time you've set. (I know we are ignoring both interest and inflation here, but a simplified calculation is fine to start with.)

4. Set up a separate fee-free savings account for each goal you have. Alternatively, you might be able to create buckets or label your money in your current savings account for different purposes. In that way, you will know exactly to which goal each dollar is assigned and how far from or close to your various targets you are.

5. Decide how much to contribute to each goal and set up a transfer into your savings account(s). Use the money you've saved from day 4. Even if you can't make the contribution needed now to reach your goal in time, just start. The first step is always the most important one. Once you've taken that step, you'll find other ways to contribute, and over time I am sure you will be able to make bigger contributions.

# Day 8

## YOUR SAVINGS RATE

**B**efore we continue, let's refute a persistent belief that you should find the magic formula that says if you're X years old you should have saved Y amount. Of course, having a bank account with $1,000,000 stashed away when you're fifty sounds blissful, but in many cases this is highly unrealistic. More important and much more workable than the amount of money you save is your savings rate: the proportion of money you save relative to your income.

I know it's tempting to use "I'm not making enough money" as an excuse not to make saving a priority, but the real power of your savings isn't about how much you save, but the percentage you save. If you are saving very small amounts and you find it demotivating to think about how little money you can save each month, then look at it this way: If you set aside 1/10 of your income each month, after one year you've bought yourself 36.5 income-free days. That's more than a month you have in savings to live on. If you manage to save only 1/20 of your income, that's still 18 days you can cover without the need to work, whereas if you manage to hit 1/5 in savings, you stash away 73 days' worth each year.

See, that's the advantage of looking at your savings rate over looking at a specific amount. As everybody has different spending patterns, having that $1,000,000 in the bank might not be the right objective to focus on if your expenses and income level are much lower anyway.

Here's another way you can see how powerful a savings rate (SR) is:

★ If you make $1,500 net a month and reach an SR of 10%, you save $150 each month and live off $1,350 for your expenses each month.

★ If, on the other hand, you get to an SR of 20%, you save $300 each month and live off $1,200.

Now let's imagine that after three years of doing this, you lose your job, and your income from one month to the next disappears. This is how the above scenarios would pan out:

★ With an SR of 10%, after three years (thirty-six months) you'd have saved $5,400. As you are used to living off $1,350, this buffer would last for four months if you need to use it as your sole source of income (assuming your expenses stay the same).

★ In the case of a 20% SR, your savings would be $10,800 after three years. As you live off $1,200 a month, you would be able to support yourself for nine months with that money.

An SR of twice as much (20% instead of 10%) would last *more* than twice as long in case of need, as an increased SR works in two ways simultaneously: not only do you save more, you also spend less.

Of course, the above picture is slightly simplified, since your savings aren't made up only of money you deposit in your savings account, but also of any contributions that you make to longer-term savings, such as your retirement account(s) or any private investment accounts you have. These, at the end of the day, also contain money you didn't spend now because you're keeping it for the future. That means those contributions would still be classified as savings, even if they aren't easily accessible in a bank account to use if your income fell away.

With that in mind, from here on, don't get too worked up about how much you earn and save, but focus on the percentage of your income you save.

## $\mathscr{Day}\ 8$ ACTION PLAN
# Determine your target savings rate and start moving toward it.

---

1. Calculate your SR for the last three months. In order to do so, you need to know your total income per month and how much you saved each month. This includes contributions to your savings, retirement, and investment accounts, as well as payments you made to pay down debt. Divide your savings by your total income, multiply the number by 100 and add a % sign to find out your SR.

2. As we saw in Part 2 of this book, your expenses and savings are closely linked. Whatever you don't spend, you can save and set to work for your future. The 50/20/30 guideline tells us to aim for 20% of your income to not be spent but to go to savings, though you also should have identified a personalized savings percentage specific to you on day 6. Let's put that objective into action by taking small steps to start working toward this.

3. Aim to increase your SR by 1% every two months (or if that is too much, by 1% every three months) until you reach the SR target you chose on day 6. Calculate how much 1% is in dollars, euros, pounds, or your own currency, and determine how you are going to hit this target every 2–3 months. What changes do you need to make now as well as long term to reach this objective? Use the ideas you brainstormed on day 6 to get you started.

# Day 9

## AUTOMATE YOUR SAVINGS

Now that you have your target SR clear from the previous task, let's ensure you achieve this rate every month by setting up automatic transfers for all of your savings contributions.

The challenge with savings is, as you've seen already, that it often gets left until the end of the month, when you find out how much is left over to contribute to savings. Throughout the month, people generally spend first and save what is left at the end. That means saving isn't given priority, and even with a spending plan, other things might get in the way of reaching savings targets.

As long as the money is in your bank account or wallet, it can be a challenge not to spend it, even if you've planned otherwise. But of course, by spending that money instead of putting it away in your savings or retirement accounts, you forfeit your own targets and resolutions.

So let's make sure you always hit the monthly savings goals you set for yourself and turn the sequence around: save first, then spend what is left over. By automating your savings payments to be taken out of your checking account at the start of each month, or right after you've been paid, your money is safely locked away, so you can't be tempted to spend it on something that wasn't in the plan—no more temptations and excuses to start saving next month instead of today.

## *Day 9* ACTION PLAN
# Direct each month's savings toward your goals.

1. Take your SR target for next month, which you determined on day 8, and decide what those savings are made up of: How much will go to each savings target?

   • If your SR is 12% for next month and your take-home pay is $1,800, then you need to save $216. Of this amount, how much will go to your savings account (or various ones, if that's the case), your investments, and your retirement fund?

2. Log in to the bank account where you receive your paycheck and set up automatic transfers into your various savings accounts. Put them down for one or two days after you receive your income, so it's taken out of your account at the start of your expense cycle. It's best not to set them for the date you normally get paid in case your employer is one or two days late paying, as that might mean risking overdrawing your bank account.

3. As you are now increasing your SR by 1% every 2–3 months, as determined on day 8, make sure to adjust your automatic payments too with the correct amount when the time comes around to increase.

# Day 10

## YOUR NET WORTH

W ould you like to get a quick overview of your financial situation, a way to see what type of condition your finances are really in, or to know how you are progressing from one month to the next?

Then knowing your net worth is a great and relatively easy way to achieve this.

Your net worth instantly shows you how healthy or unhealthy your finances are and whether you have an overall favorable balance sheet or not. It also gives you an easy way to set targets, to see how your situation improves from one month to the next, and to gain an overview of how the various areas that make up your financial health link together.

Your net worth can be either positive or negative and, simply put, tells you what your financial situation would be if you first sold all of your possessions and second paid off all of your debts. If your net worth is positive, you own more than you owe, which means you'd still have money left over. If, on the other hand, your net worth is negative, you have more debts than possessions, meaning you wouldn't be able to pay off all your debts even if you sold all of what you own.

If you're like most people who are starting off on a journey to improve their financial lives, you'll more than likely have a negative net worth. And I don't mean negative in the sense of -$2,000, but likely more toward tens of thousands of negative dollars, especially if you have a mortgage or big student loan of which you haven't yet paid off much.

Don't get discouraged by such an amount, but use it as a motivation to turn this figure into a positive one. Once you've calculated your net worth for the first time, it will be easy to keep doing so on a regular basis, so getting a monthly overview will be simple and helpful to keep you on track.

## *Day 10* ACTION PLAN
# Determine your net worth.

1. Make a list of everything you own at a significant level: house, savings accounts, investments, and life insurance if applicable, along with the approximate value of each. Don't worry about cars, jewelry, antiques, or art unless you know they are worth a lot.

2. Now list all your current outstanding debts: mortgage, student loan, auto loan, and credit card balance.

3. Subtract the total amount of debts from the total value of possessions to find your net worth.

4. Write down your current net worth along with today's date. Make it a habit to recalculate your net worth each month. Set a specific target for your net worth if this helps you. As your net worth is a generic total of all of your financial areas together, it doesn't specify which of those areas you'd like to focus on (investments, paying down debt, savings, etc.) to achieve that goal, but it can still be helpful to have an overall goal to get a global feel of your financial progress.

# YOUR DEBTS

After working on your mindset, expenses, and savings, let's move on to look at your debts. If you have a significant amount of debt, you might feel there is no way out, and you might even prefer not to think about this topic at all. Or you might have given up on the idea of ever becoming debt-free and accepted that outstanding loans are an integral part of your life and, indeed, our society.

If any of that's the case, then rest assured you're not the only one. More importantly, though, I intend to change these beliefs in the coming section.

Let's start with why having debt seems so normal these days. There are, broadly speaking, two reasons we accumulate debt and spend before we have the money. First, some purchases are so enormously expensive—think about a house, for example—that it is nearly impossible to get all the money together before buying it.

Or if you did, you might need to wait until you're in your fifties or sixties before you could buy your first house!

The second reason is less practical and has more to do with the inability to control desire: we want the latest gadget, a bigger car, a more exotic holiday. And we want them all now, not tomorrow. We've become so accustomed to wanting more, and— partially because we see others around us with things we too wish to have, and partially because we might believe we have earned or deserved to acquire those things—we care less about the financial implications of purchasing them than instantly gratifying our wants.

If that means taking out a loan or using a credit card and worrying about how to pay back those loans later (along with all the extra interest and personal stress that might come with that effort), then so be it. That's just part of life, right?

Having debt, and buying something before having the money to pay for it, seems to have become the default for many people and, indeed, for society as a whole. We see having debt as a standard way of life. But simply because others have debt, doesn't mean it's the best option to pursue. Having debt costs money, causes stress, ties you to your creditors, and might keep you in a job you don't enjoy, because you need to pay all those creditors.

Wouldn't it be much healthier, cheaper, more satisfying, and a lot less stressful if you were able to save up for those purchases before buying them? Imagine how powerful you would feel knowing you were able to plan and save for something first. Now that would really be earning something! (You might exclude a long-term investment in an asset, like that house I mentioned before, or setting up a company, which can be too expensive to pay for in cash up front.)

From today onward, I want you to set yourself an important goal: to become completely debt-free. Sound like too big a mountain to climb? Remember that as long as you have debts, you spend money on interest and compounding interest, which can make the payback cycle incredibly long and expensive. By becoming debt-free, you will no longer waste money on loans for things you might have purchased months or years ago. Once you pay off your very last debt, you will free up a substantial part of your cash flow to build a secure financial future instead of paying off past purchases. You can live without wondering how you're going to pay off the overdue bills hidden away in a shoebox under the bed.

Last, if you do ever need to take out a loan, such as for a big purchase like a house, you're not only much more likely to qualify for it, but also could get one with better conditions. The more responsible you show you can be with money (e.g., by not have lots of outstanding debts), the more likely you will be able to pay back your mortgage, and the less of a risk you are to a bank, meaning they are more likely to grant you the mortgage and offer it at a lower interest rate.

# Day 11

## GAIN CLARITY ON YOUR DEBTS

**D**ebt can come in several forms: a student loan, a mortgage, a car loan, medical bills, credit card balances, or a personal loan from a friend or family member.

I am guessing you've probably got a debt or two (or three or four) that at times give you the cold sweats during the day or night when you're wondering how you're ever going to pay them off.

Well, that's exactly what we'll be looking at in the next four days. The only way to finally eradicate debt from your life is by ceasing to ignore it or be passive. Running away from it, not opening statements, or brushing everything under the carpet will not make that debt go away, nor will it stop you from thinking about it. The only thing this behavior achieves is that instead of having productive thoughts about your debt to help you plan how to pay it off, you suppress those thoughts and feelings, which leads to them brooding underneath the surface, causing stress and anxiety as you don't know what to do with them or how to proactively work toward a solution.

If you've ever thought it impossible to pursue a debt-free life, you'd better get used to the idea that this is precisely what you'll be aiming at from here on. Gone are the days of sticking your head in the sand and ignoring your debt or not having a plan to become debt-free. In order to get there, let's start with your current situation and gain clarity on how much debt you have.

As you put together a full picture of your debts, be thorough and don't leave anything out. Include any money you owe to others, even if it is a small amount or a personal loan from family.

### *Day 11* ACTION PLAN
# Know what you owe.

1. Collect statements from every possible debt you have. Find the latest paper bill, log in to your account, or contact the company you owe money to for the latest balances. You might have gathered some of this information on day 10 to calculate your net worth.

2. List all your debts, and note down their outstanding balances, interest rates, remaining life spans, and minimum monthly payments.

3. Have a look at your list. For a moment, let any feelings and thoughts flow, which might include fear about your spending habits, worries about how you are going to pay these off, alarm at how much you owe, relief at how little it is, excitement about finally committing to eliminating them from your life, or anything else.

4. That's all for today. On day 12, we'll look at what to do next, but for now, reward yourself with a little treat, knowing you've taken the first grand step toward becoming debt-free.

# Day 12

## PAY OFF YOUR DEBTS

t's time to get real and start to eliminate debt from your life. In order to do so, you need to start doing two things: don't get into any more debt, and make paying off your current debts a priority.

Let's start with not taking on any more loans and debts. That means there'll be no more whipping out your credit card if you don't have the money in your bank account to pay it off each and every month. If needed, cut up or store away credit cards so you won't be tempted.

Becoming debt-free doesn't mean you can't get that new gadget or redesign your kitchen; it just means you save up the money before you purchase it. This might involve some planning (and patience). If you completed the savings section of this book, you should by now have set up different savings targets and accounts to which you contribute money for future expenses you envision. This means by the time you need to make those purchases, you shouldn't need to take on a loan, as you would have the money saved up in a bank account if you planned well.

After you've committed to not taking on any more debt, let's make paying off your current debt a priority. By paying down your debts faster, you save a lot of money on compounding interest (interest charged on interest) as well as stress and time spent on the debt itself. Here's a quick example to illustrate how much of a difference paying off your debts might make:

If you had a $1,000 credit card loan at a 1.5% monthly interest rate and an agreed payment plan of 3% per month (meaning each month you pay back 3% of the outstanding balance you owe) with a minimum of $10, you would pay back the incredible amount of $779 in interest in total on this loan! Not only that, it would also take you nine years and ten months to pay off this loan.

Let's imagine you were able to pay an extra $25 each month in addition to the minimum payment you must make to your credit card company, you would pay only $221 in interest—over $550 less interest than the $779! Added to that, with the extra $25 a month you pay, it would take you just thirty-one months to pay off the loan (a little over two and a half years) instead of the 118 months it would take you with just the minimum payment.

As you can see, making even small extra payments is worth it when it comes to paying off your debts. When putting together your debt payment plan, you can choose between two strategies: the snowball or the avalanche technique.

With the **snowball technique**, you start with the smallest debt you have and begin to pay down this debt as fast as you can. In the meantime, you keep making the minimum contributions to any other debts you have. You don't want to accumulate any penalties for defaulting on these payments, after all. Once that first loan is paid off, move on to the next-smallest debt and pay off the minimum amount you were already paying plus the money freed up from the first debt. The advantage of the snowball technique is that you see results very early on. The smaller the debt, the quicker you can pay it off, meaning you gain momentum quickly.

In the **avalanche technique**, you begin paying off the debt with the highest interest rate. This is, ultimately, the one that over time accrues the highest amount of interest on it, so by paying this one off first you save a lot of money in the long run. As in the snowball technique, make sure to continue making the minimum contributions to any other debts you have while you pay off your highest-interest one. Once the highest-interest loan is paid off, move on to the next one, using the extra money you have freed up from the first debt to add to the minimum payments for the next one.

## *Day 12* ACTION PLAN
# Snowball or avalanche, get that debt rolling away.

1. Decide whether you want to use the snowball or avalanche technique. This is a personal preference. Both options have pros and cons, so do what feels right for you and makes sense with the various debts you have.

2. Look at the list of debts you made on day 11 and identify the debt to pay back first: the smallest one in the case of the snowball technique, the one with the highest interest rate with the avalanche approach.

3. Determine how much money you can pay extra each month toward your first debt on top of all the minimum payments you are making. Once again, don't underestimate the power of small numbers!

4. Set up an automatic transfer to pay the extra amount of money on that first debt.

5. Update your spending plan to account for the extra money you're using to pay off your debt.

6. Make sure to stick to your minimum payments on all your other loans. Don't default on them or you'll be charged extra fees, canceling out all the effort you're making on paying off your other debt.

7. Once you've paid off one debt, use all the money you used to pay for that debt to start paying off your next loan. Keep doing this until you've paid off your very last loan.

# Day 13

## PLAN TO BECOME DEBT-FREE

Unfortunately, there's nothing easier than falling back into old habits once the novelty of a new project or resolution has worn off—even when you are completely charged up and feel 100% dedicated at the start.

Today's task is all about avoiding such a backslide. And you'll do this by setting up a plan to back up your commitment to becoming debt-free. Putting an idea in writing with very clear milestones and targets makes it much more real and increases your chance of success exponentially. That means putting together a plan with practical, achievable, and motivating outcomes that support your overall goal.

**Here's what such a plan should include:**

★ The list of debts from day 11, organized from first to last, based on which one you'll pay off first, second, etc.

★ The amount of extra money you decided to throw at your first debt monthly.

★ How long it will take you to pay the debt you'll be tackling first. Use an online calculator to work this out, as you'll likely have interest compounding on that debt, so it isn't a simple math sum.

★ An *estimated* date for when you'll pay off each individual debt. Make them stand out so reaching each goal will be worth a celebration! You can add a champagne bottle or festive emoji to your e-calendar, or put a note with the date in double bold with funky colors or highlights up on your fridge, or as your screensaver. The further down the road, the more money you'll have available to pay off each debt, as each time you eradicate a debt, the monthly payment you made on that debt becomes available to use on the next one. With time you'll speed up your payments, but due to compounding interest and other unexpected financial events that might happen in terms of your spending plan, don't worry about calculating the end date for all of your debts completely. You can update these dates regularly, but having an estimated finish date gives you a good starting point that can be refined later.

★ The date for paying off your very last debt will be your estimated date for when you become completely debt-free. Put this in an even bigger font in your calendar.

## *Day 13* ACTION PLAN
# Set your calendar for debt freedom.

1. Using the list from day 11 with all the details of your various debts and taking into account the extra money you can pay each month, use an online calculator to work out when you'll be paying off each and every one of your other debts. Put these dates somewhere noticeable so they act as reminders.

2. Put a reminder in your digital calendar to update these dates every three months to account for small changes that might happen—such as an extra payment you make toward a debt, compounding interest, or a change in interest rates—to keep them as accurate as possible.

3. Make the most important estimated date—when you'll pay off your very last debt and become debt-free—stand out even more. That will be one of the most important achievements on your way to financial excellence.

# Day 14

## BUILD AN EMERGENCY FUND

A s you're setting yourself up to slowly become debt-free, let's ensure you can stay that way after that date arrives, even in light of possible setbacks.

If you've ever had your washing machine break down, your car need an instant repair, or your pet require an emergency operation, then you know how difficult it can be to not go into debt when you face unexpected events. These unplanned but highly urgent expenses can easily throw you off balance and make you dip into your savings or incur more debt to pay for them. Let's not allow that to happen again.

I know you can't plan for these expenses per se, as they are unexpected by their very nature, but you *can* plan for the unplanned as a general strategy. The simple solution is to have cash set aside specifically to cover emergencies when they happen. So even if you don't yet know what the emergency will be, at least you will be prepared to deal with it.

Of course, the principal objective of an emergency fund is to be able to deal with an unexpected expense for something you can't do without. It isn't to fund fun things like a trip you are invited on by your best friend or to buy a new phone just because you fancy one. These should be things you save up for over time—keep the emergency fund for what it is truly for: emergencies.

You can save up for your emergency fund in several ways; here are some ideas to get you started:

★ Use whatever money you are saving from the expenses you cut in day 4.

★ Boost your fund by clearing out your garage or attic and selling stuff others might be interested in on eBay or Craigslist.

★ Make extra money by picking up extra hours at work or starting a side hustle that can bring in some money quickly (see also day 16).

## *Day 14* ACTION PLAN
## Get ready for the unexpected.

1. Aim to set up an emergency fund of $1,000 (or the equivalent in your own currency).

2. Keep your emergency fund in a cost-free savings account separate from your other accounts to avoid the temptation of using it for something else.

3. Use the ideas above or whatever other idea you have to start building this fund. The sooner you get your fund together, the more peace you'll feel knowing that if anything happens, you've got a few dollars set aside to cover the immediate costs.

4. If you ever need to use some of your emergency money (and you likely will at some point), aim to top it back up to its original amount as soon as you can afterward.

# YOUR INCOME

The income section you're about to start with is in some ways the most exciting part of this 30-day financial plan. It presents a close look at the many options to earn income, and it can be thrilling to think about possible ways to take home a little more money each month!

It is not uncommon for people to think their income is what it is and that, apart from getting a raise, there's not much one can do to make more money. This is, however, a flawed assumption, one which disregards your influence on and accountability for the amount of money you earn. It makes you a passive receiver of your boss's financial decision and ignores not only your power to become more indispensable to your company and negotiate a higher income, but more importantly, it ignores your potential to start a private venture and supplement whatever your job pays with something that is in the realm of your own power.

Your income tomorrow needn't remain the same as what it is today and can be influenced by you. In particular—and this is the most inspiring thing about income—you can have more than one income stream, meaning you can earn money from more than just one source. This doesn't automatically mean working two jobs. It means creating something on the side that adds to your wages. Having more than one source of income is a tremendously empowering and motivating feat to accomplish.

**With a variety of income streams you:**

★ Have a safety net in case you lose your job.

★ Have more control over how much you earn.

★ Have more control over when and where you work.

★ Earn more money.

Here's the thing: if you control your money sources, you control your future. At the end of the day, you never know what will happen at your job. You might get fired, be made redundant (laid off), be transferred to another department, or simply want to quit if you reach a point where you no longer enjoy it. By taking charge of your income, you can direct your future and what exactly it will look like.

Once you begin looking at your total income as being controlled by *you*, it can become an adventure to see how to increase your income each month. This is a very powerful solution to resolving your financial worries. Ultimately, you can cut down your expenses only so much, but when it comes to your income, there aren't any limits.

# Day 15

## DETERMINE YOUR INCOME

To start taking control over your income, you're once again going to take stock of your current situation by mapping out how much income you get in each of the seven different income streams.

"Wait, what? Seven?" Yes, there are seven types of income streams, and income from a job is just one of them! We'll quickly look at those seven streams of income here, even if you've got only one. Some of these might provide a negligible amount of income while others might seem completely unattainable at this moment. Just bear with me for now, as they might give you some ideas for future income projects.

1. **Earned income from a job:** This is any money you earn through your work for a company. This income stream is generally based on getting paid for your time.

2. **Profit:** The money you make by selling products or services as part of a business activity at a higher price than the cost. This could be anything from design work or furniture to homemade dog clothing or jewelry you create.

3. **Royalties:** Money you receive on products you have made or from franchises of your brand. This can be from music, books, artwork used for postcards or wallpaper, or knitting patterns sold to yarn companies, to name just a few.

4. **Interest income:** Money you get from lending money to others, such as to a bank or the government through investments. Examples include interest on your savings account or bonds.

5. **Dividend income:** Money you get from shares in an investment portfolio if the company whose shares you own makes a profit they can pay out.

6. **Capital gains:** Any money you receive as a result of selling something you acquired at a cheaper price than what you are selling it for. These typically include art, antiques, and real estate.

7. **Rental income:** The rent you collect from renting out assets you own. While this is usually property, it can also be on a smaller scale, such as a car or lawn mower.

## $\mathcal{D}ay$ 15 ACTION PLAN
## Identify your income streams.

1. Make a list of the seven income streams and write down your monthly income in each area. Make sure to include those streams that have no income, as those might be options for the future.

2. If your income varies each month, write down the average from the last six months.

3. Be consistent and write down either the gross (pretax) or the net (after-tax) amount.

4. Regardless whether you went for the gross or net amount, find out the tax rates for each income stream and write them next to the source of income. Most countries have different types of income taxes for different categories, so it's worth finding out what they are. In all likelihood, $100 gross earned through a job will result in a different net amount than $100 earned through dividends. This might help you decide which income stream to expand in the future.

# Day 16

## START A SIDE HUSTLE

Apart from the many advantages having a job might give you, including a sense of purpose, helping others, sharing your expertise, a social network, an income (not unimportant!), and other financial benefits such as insurance and retirement provisions that might come with it, there are also possible disadvantages of having to depend on others, such as the conditions of your salary increases, the continuation of your contract, your duties and the projects you get assigned, and the hours of work you are required to put in.

By relying on just one source of income, you are making yourself vulnerable to market changes, company policies, and, ultimately, others determining your work conditions and earnings.

I'm a big advocate of adding to your regular income an income stream that you are much more in control of. A side hustle doesn't need to be a full-fledged business. It can have all the flexibility in the world and might involve dedicating only a few hours a week or even a month whenever you wish. Most importantly, it makes you more financially independent, meaning that even if you lost your job (or chose not to continue), you'd still have at least some alternative income stream that brings in money, which you might at that point be able to scale up. And the more money you get from it, the less you need to rely on just your wages to provide for yourself and your family.

But where do you start? This is where the seven income streams come in particularly useful, as they allow you to break down the options more easily. And as your job is, of course, one of the seven types of income, let's also look at ways to increase earnings there.

Before we have a closer look at the seven options, however, bear in mind that some of them are more appropriate for creating another income stream years or even decades in the future rather than in the short term. In particular, dividend income, capital gains, and rental income from a property require up-front capital and involve long-term turnover between when you start investing and when you can get money out; they don't instantly provide you with extra cash. I therefore highly recommend you first save up your emergency fund, pay off your debts, and save for more immediate savings goals, as well as consider more short-term ways to create a side hustle (through profit or royalty streams) before you start thinking about creating income streams for the long haul.

1.  **Earned income from a job:** Up your monthly earnings or increase the likelihood of a bonus by finding ways to become more indispensable, pursue a promotion, or consider getting a better-paying job.

2.  **Profit:** Start a side hustle selling things you make or offering your services, such as an Etsy shop, tutoring, or a specialized IT service.

3.  **Royalties:** Write a book, compose music, or design stationery, wallpaper, or new software.

4.  **Interest income:** Increase your savings, your investment in bonds, or your crowdfunding contributions.

5.  **Dividend income:** Buy (more) shares to increase the amount of dividend earnings.

6.  **Capital gains:** Invest (more) in the stock market, houses, or antiques to build up a bigger portfolio with the aim to sell later on when those assets have appreciated.

7.  **Rental income:** Buy property in order to rent it out or consider smaller-scale options, such as renting out baby products, a drill, and other items.

When going through the list, start with what you enjoy doing: When are the moments you are totally absorbed in something and forget about time, your surroundings, or what's for dinner tonight . . . times when you are completely present in the moment? That might well be your thing. Do something with it. Explore options for using that to help others and turn it into something others would want to pay for.

## *Day 16* ACTION PLAN
# Get started on your side hustle.

1. Brainstorm initial ideas that come to mind regarding a possible side hustle. Write them down, even if at this point they sound crazy to you. Here are some more ideas if you're still struggling.

   - Pick up jobs on the side: do hourly gigs like babysitting, housesitting, dog walking, or tutoring.

   - Build a profit income: offer services or goods to a wider audience; start a blog, create an online course, or start a consultancy in your area of specialty.

   - Turn a hobby into a profit or royalty income: write, draw, paint, or craft and sell your goods on Etsy or at the local art gallery, or find an agent to represent you.

   - Consider whether you want to focus on increasing your wages at work instead of starting a side hustle, and brainstorm ways to do so.

2. Thinking about initial costs, the time you have available, the enjoyment you'd get out of each new project, and the possibility of actually making money with it, decide on one hustle option you can commit to at this point.

3. Write down the first few steps you need to complete to get started. Then begin the first step and mark your calendar with its projected completion date.

4. Every time you complete a step, start the next task on the list and also add another step to the bottom of the list, so you always know where you are going. Plan in time each week to work on your side hustle.

# Day 17

## SET YOUR INCOME GOAL

I n the last two days, we've looked at your regular source of income as well as possible new side hustles to supplement that income. Now it's time to set yourself a goal for what you'd want your income to be. We'd all like to make more money, so why not start actively pursuing this vision? I want you to set a new, big income goal—one that seems intimidating but also very exciting. Think about it this way: if you don't prioritize to earn the wages you want to earn and get paid for the value you add (both inside and outside your regular job), then nobody will. Get used to acknowledging to yourself that it's okay to pursue the money you want to earn, not the money you happen to be earning at the moment, so you can take care of yourself and your loved ones.

In today's action plan, you will set your own target, whether that's $5,000 a month or double the amount you're earning now. It is completely up to you. If you don't know where to start, begin by taking your current yearly income and adding on 25%. That will be your starting point and your target to be making in a year's time. If this sounds like a scary jump from what you are earning now, then you've got it right! You don't want to set a small goal here that you know you're going to achieve anyway. If it doesn't sound that scary to you, then add another 25% or 50% until you feel it's enough above your current wages to get a little nervous in terms of how you'd possibly make that happen.

Alternatively, if you are gravitating toward having more time instead of more money, your target can be to earn exactly what you're earning now *but by working 25% fewer hours.* That, of course, is okay too if that's your underlying motivation.

The next step is to decide how you are going to make this increase in income a reality. Will it all come from a side hustle? An increase in your salary? Plan out how you'll be getting to your income target in just one year. Set out smaller targets along the way to achieve (e.g., monthly) so that you can monitor your progress and hold yourself accountable.

Getting more money is no longer optional. From here on, you'll be working diligently every week toward your new income goal. You might need to try out different things or do more than one thing at the same time; this might mean facing your boss to ask for a raise, looking and applying for a new job, and starting that gig on the side. Getting started is what counts. You got this!

## *Day 17* ACTION PLAN
## Create the conditions to earn scary money.

1. Set your income goal for next year. Write down the actual number; don't just have a vague percentage in your head. If it isn't big and scary or seemingly unattainable at this stage, then it's not big enough.

2. Now write down next to it the date one year from today.

3. Identify where exactly this extra money will be coming from. Be specific as to how much will come from your job and how much from your side hustle.

4. Once you've identified the various sources of your total income, work out how you're going to work on each source individually. What do you need to do in each area to achieve this?

5. As with some of the other tasks, put the key information where you'll see it every day, and make it a habit to regularly update your progress on each income goal you have set yourself every month.

# Day 18

YOUR PERSONAL CAPITAL

Your knowledge, experience, and skills make you unique. Nobody else comes with the same bag of experience, insights, and abilities. That one-of-a-kind combination is your personal capital, and it is your single biggest asset that enables you to make money, be that at your job or at your side hustle. It is what makes you *you* and different from all others when it comes to adding value to the world.

To conserve your personal capital as your greatest good, you need to look after it well and nurture it with what it needs. That requires regularly investing in it so you can continue to develop, allowing you to keep an edge over others and to expand your knowledge.

Whether you feed your personal capital with new information, skills, or experience, learning something new can be really fun; it stimulates the mind, and it can be intriguing to think about the possible projects or perspectives it can give you.

In this day and age, it is simpler than ever before to invest in your personal capital: there are books available on pretty much any topic you want, while conferences and traditional courses of study as well as online training courses provide more in-depth ways to internalize new material and expand your wisdom.

But this isn't only about knowledge. In these wise words, often (mis) attributed to Einstein, "The only source of knowledge is experience. Without experience, everything else is just information."

Experience can also come in many different forms: by trying something out yourself, by working with somebody else who already masters a certain technique, or even by looking outside your own field to volunteer or interact with new people.

I highly recommend setting aside a part of your income each month to invest in your personal capital. This could be as little as $5 so you can purchase a new book on a specific topic every three to four months, or it could be as much as $50 to save up for a specific training course you want to attend. The options are endless!

## *Day 18* ACTION PLAN
## Start investing in your personal capital.

1. Make a list of things you'd like to know more about, struggle with, or are simply interested in that are related to your job or your (newly identified) side hustle.

2. Pick one project to begin with and decide what would be the best way to get started on this. Often books provide the most accessible and cheapest option to dive into a new topic, but look around for courses and traineeships, or start with free options such as blog posts, podcasts, or webinars to get a feel for what is out there.

3. Keep a running wish list of books, courses, and conferences you can add to on the go so you never run out of ideas on how to keep your personal capital at the top of your priority list.

4. Set up a personal capital category in your spending plan and determine how much to assign to this each month.

# YOUR RETIREMENT

When you think of your retirement, do you fantasize about picking up a new hobby? Spending more time with your (grand) children? Visiting long-lost friends from your past? Traveling to places you've never been to?

Or do you worry your income will be so meager that it seems impossible you can live out those dreams you've always wanted when you'll finally have time? Or is your prospect to keep working until you no longer can because you don't have the funds to support yourself otherwise?

If a comfortable retirement doesn't seem to be within your reach, then it's time to start working on your provisions now so you'll have a fun and secure retirement to look forward to.

Of course, if you are still decades away from retirement, you might be asking yourself why you need to worry about it now and whether this can't wait until you're a little older. You might also be lucky and live in a country where the state will provide you with a retirement provision, making you wonder even more whether all of this is really needed.

Here are two important reasons why you shouldn't hold off retirement planning any longer:

First, the earlier you invest in your retirement, the faster your investments will grow long term, as you'll have much more compounding interest generating more and more funds on their own for you over time. A thousand dollars invested yearly for thirty years at a 6% investment return will lead to approximately $84,000 in funds. But if you started twenty years later and invested three times the amount ($3,000 instead of $1,000), in just a third of that time (ten years instead of thirty years), this would give you only about $42,000. The true magic of compounding interest is time, not the amount of money paid in, so the earlier you start, the better.

Second, there's the issue of our population changing: We're living longer with every generation, and we have fewer children to carry the load of pensions. Therefore, social security, in particular, will likely undergo far-reaching changes, with a higher minimum state pension age and a lower monthly payout rate.

If you'd rather determine the conditions of your retirement yourself and not wait to see what you end up with and which dreams you can and can't live out, then let's get started with you taking your retirement into your own hands.

# Day 19

## TAKE STOCK OF YOUR RETIREMENT

W hat do you know about your current retirement provision? Are you aware of how much you've saved up and will likely receive by the time you retire? If you don't have a clue as to whether you are on track to hit your retirement targets or not, if you've never even set those targets, or if you have no provisions in place, then we're going to resolve this today and get started making sure your retirement will be all set!

Retirement options generally come in three formats:

★ **Social security or state pension:** Provided by the government, this is often based on years worked. If you live somewhere where this type of retirement funding exists, then during your active work life you or your employer paid taxes to fund this type of retirement provision.

★ **Workplace retirement provision:** Provided by your employer, this type of retirement fund, called a 401(k) in the US, is generally voluntary so you can opt to pay into your retirement fund or not. In some cases, your employer might match your contributions, meaning they would add money to this fund based on what you are paying in.

★ **Individual retirement account (IRA):** Often made available by banks, insurance companies, or investment companies, an individual retirement fund, such as a Roth IRA in the US, is completely at your discretion to contribute to. As there are many different companies offering IRAs, you can choose the one you see as most fitting for your situation.

Whether or not you have access to all of the above options might depend on where you live and your type of job.

## Day 19 ACTION PLAN
## Look ahead to your projected retirement income.

1. Find out about your country's or state's current social security or state pension options. What is the monthly payout, what are the conditions (such as minimum number of years worked), and what is the current as well as projected minimum pension age by the time you reach retirement age?

2. Check whether you have any retirement fund options available through your employer. If you are already contributing, check how much you have in this fund and how much this would give you by the time you retire. Find out whether your employer matches your contributions and what the conditions are for this.

3. If you have an IRA, find out how much you've paid into that fund up until now, look up the costs you're liable to incur and any specific conditions of the fund. Your current pension provider should be able to indicate your projected amount of money by the time you retire based on what you currently have paid in.

4. Now total the projected retirement funding you'd get at retirement age based on the different retirement funds you have access to. Is this more or less than what you think you'd need?

# Day 20

## SET RETIREMENT GOALS

L et's go back to the thought experiment we looked at in the introduction to this part and take a moment to picture your retirement. Really picture it. Close your eyes and think about how you would like to spend your time when you reach retirement age. Is there anything you've always wanted to do in life but have never been able to? Give yourself some time to think of what would make a gratifying retirement for you.

Once you've got a clearer idea, put your thoughts on paper. You might have one principal thing you came up with; maybe there are three important projects or areas in your life you would like to spend time on; or maybe there are a lot of smaller things. Put them in writing.

Now try as best you can to estimate what your lifestyle in retirement would cost you. How much money do you need for each project you want to focus on? And, of course, don't forget about your regular expenses, such as groceries and utilities. At the same time, you might be able to cut out certain costs by the time you retire, such as your mortgage payments, work-related costs, and maybe even contributions you are making to retirement funds.

Taking all your expenses together, estimate how much you'd need on a monthly basis to live that lifestyle. Is it much more than your current monthly expenses? A lot less? Similar?

Depending on your pictured retirement and the retirement funds you currently have set up that we looked at on day 19, you might realize that your ideal retirement is much more expensive than you thought. In that case, you might need to have a reality check and scale down your ideas a little to make them more realistic.

At the same time, I don't want you to discard all your dreams either, as it can be exciting to dream and build on your plans. So make sure to hold on to at least some of your aspirations and get planning on how to make them happen!

Before we continue, a small note on inflation seems needed, as that will likely have a big impact on your retirement planning, especially if you are still several decades away from your retirement. To be on the safe side, count on 3% inflation per year to add to your yearly needs, meaning that if you think you can live off $18,000 a year, you should add an extra $540 next year due to the loss in value money will experience. In 25 years' time, that $18,000 will actually be nearly $(1.03)^{25} \times \$18,000 = \$37,700$! Check with your pension provider about whether their projected numbers take inflation into account or not.

## $\mathcal{D}ay$ 20 ACTION PLAN
## Know today's steps to finance your dream retirement of tomorrow.

1. Estimate the amount of money you'd need on a monthly basis to support your retirement dreams.

2. From day 19's task, you should have a good idea of how much you will be getting by the time you retire based on your current retirement savings and contributions. How far away from your target monthly retirement income are you?

3. How much would you need to set aside each month from now on to close that gap between your projected and your desired retirement income? Use an online calculator or check with your retirement account provider to find this out.

# Day 21

## INCREASE YOUR CONTRIBUTIONS AND CLOSE YOUR RETIREMENT GAP

From the work you've done the last two days, you should now have a clear picture of what you'd *like* your retirement to look like, as well as what it most likely *will* look like, based on your current setup. In today's task, we're going to use that information to actively plan out your retirement and try to bridge the gap between your ideal and your likely retirement picture.

In order to do so, you'll need to make the most of the various options available to you. If you might be entitled to a retirement fund provided by the state, you have, of course, little control over its conditions and the contributions you make. But what you can do is to make sure you don't miss out on this money if it is within easy reach. Most countries that offer social security will have a condition that you need to have worked for a certain number of years at minimum to claim full benefits. This is worth bearing in mind, for example, if you are considering giving up a job or becoming a full-time homemaker.

Second, if you have a retirement fund offered by your employer, you should know from day 19's task whether they match your contributions and what the conditions are. Your employer might match up to 4%, for example, meaning that any contributions you make to your fund, your employer would match up to a limit of 4% of your salary. If your yearly wages are

$40,000 and you pay 4% ($1,600) of this toward your retirement fund, your employer would pay in the same amount. If you paid in more, the contribution from your employer would still be capped at $1,600; if you paid in just $1,200, your employer would, of course, also pay in only $1,200. Your employer's matching program is free money you can get, and if you aren't yet making the most of it, this might be one of the first areas in which you may wish to increase your contributions.

If you are already maxing out your employer's retirement fund, or don't have access to one, then you should look into opening an IRA with an investment or insurance company or a bank. An IRA means you need to make more decisions in terms of which type of fund to invest in, but it also means you have more control over your retirement and that you can choose a plan that best suits your profile.

Once you have your IRA, or if you want to participate in a 401(k) at work, you need to find ways to make contributions. Start by making the minimum required contributions for now, but aim to increase this by a certain percentage each year. Additionally, when you free up some money, such as by paying off your last debt, or if your income increases, make sure to direct at least 50% of it to your pension fund.

## *Day 21* ACTION PLAN
## Boost your retirement income now.

1. Decide how much you can realistically currently pay into your retirement account. Don't get discouraged if this isn't a lot because, as before, even small (extra) payments will make a difference long term and will also get you into the habit of making increases whenever you can. Adjust your spending plan to account for this payment.

2. If you aren't doing so already and have access to a workplace retirement fund, set up automatic transfers into your 401(k)

and work toward maxing out contributions to your employer's retirement fund if they are matching it.

3. If you don't have the option to participate in a workplace retirement fund, if your employer doesn't match your contributions, or if you're maxing that out already, look into IRA options, then compare conditions, open an account that best meets your needs, and set up automatic transfers into this fund.

4. Mark a date in your calendar to review your retirement fund contributions and whether you can increase them further. To get started, aim for an increase of $10 every three months (or more if you can).

5. Keep track of your retirement funds and check how much closer you are to your retirement dreams each year. Make adjustments where possible to get a step closer to these dreams.

# Day 22

## INVEST IN YOUR OWN PORTFOLIO

The great advantage of funding your retirement accounts (over, for example, investing in an investment portfolio) isn't just that you invest in your financial future, but also that you often get a tax advantage. This generally happens in one of two ways:

- ★ **Applying a tax advantage when you pay in:** Your contributions are taken from your gross wages, meaning before you pay your income tax. This results in a higher amount contributed and is often the case with workplace retirement accounts.

- ★ **Applying a tax advantage when you withdraw:** Your withdrawals from your account by the time you are retired are tax-free. This means you keep all the money instead of paying income tax on it; this often applies to IRAs.

So, while retirement funds can be a great way to invest in a secure future, they are also subject to limitations. Your retirement contributions are normally invested in the stock market to make them grow for you over time, but in most cases you also have little to no say in how this money is invested. That means your money might not be getting the best returns possible, leaving you with less money than you could get.

Additionally, the money you invest now you are not allowed to spend whenever you want: you can generally only get access again when you reach retirement age, and unless you're willing to pay hefty fines, there are only a few exceptions to this, such as in cases of serious, often health-related situations.

A third limitation of both Roth IRAs and a 401(k) fund is that they have a yearly limit of how much you can invest in them. These limits are relatively high, but once you reach them you will need another alternative if you want to invest more money.

A good option is to invest money yourself in a private investment portfolio. This is an attractive way to add yet another (long-term) side income of possible dividends and interest to your earnings. But even more importantly, it allows you to build up assets for the future that can give capital gains as an addition to your retirement funds.

While investing may sound intimidating, it needn't be if you inform yourself well. The full details are well beyond the scope of this book, but let's at least have a quick look at what investing entails. To put it simply, you can invest either in shares (tiny parts of a company) or bonds (loans companies take out and then pay back later).

The easiest and cheapest way to invest, and also generally the option that involves less risk, is to invest in index funds, which means that you follow a particular index (a collection of companies that trade on the market, such as the S&P 500, the Dow Jones, or the Nasdaq) and invest in a wide range of their most successful companies. With this investing strategy you don't need to choose how much to invest in which company specifically. The investing fund will decide this for you based on which companies make up the index and what their relative size is within the index.

You can also handpick stocks and decide on just a few companies you want to invest in. While a third alternative is to invest in mutual funds managed by a funds manager. Both of these last two ways are generally more expensive due to extra fees, and these portfolios are also more risky and volatile (meaning their prices can go up and down more and faster so you can experience greater wins *and* greater losses), as they are based on trying to predict what the stock market will be doing—something that, as countless studies and experts have indicated, isn't actually possible. Index investing is a much more low-key way to invest and can often be done for as little as $50–$100 a month.

While investing in your own portfolio doesn't offer the tax advantages you get from pension funds you invest in, it does give you extra flexibility when it comes to deciding what to invest in and especially when to start drawing from this fund, as you don't need to wait until reaching retirement age to do so. It is certainly worth looking into investing as a way to build another small set of assets on the side that you can turn into cash with time, once you've made sufficient progress with your savings, your retirement funds, and paying down debt!

Bear in mind, however, that investing is never without risk, and that markets can both soar and plummet within a matter of weeks or even days. Don't put all your savings in an investment account; spread the risk and make sure to educate yourself about the basics before you get started.

## 𝒟𝑎𝑦 22 ACTION PLAN
## Start or increase your investments.

1. Investing is never without risk. Find a good resource to learn more about investing before you take the plunge. There are a lot of books, articles, and tutorials you can read or watch online. Or have a look at the step-by-step-investing section of my book *100 Steps to Financial Independence*.

2. Look at your spending plan and decide whether you are currently able to invest a small amount each month. See if you can free up money, or whether you need to stick with other financial targets first, such as paying off your debts or building an emergency fund, before investing. Investing is a long-term project, and I highly recommend that you build a secure financial basis before you start

investing. Don't worry if you aren't ready to do this yet; you might be in a year or two, which is fine.

3. If you are keen to start investing, investigate some options, read reviews of different investment companies, make sure you are aware of any costs and minimum payments, and then open an account. Set up an automatic monthly contribution and update your spending plan. Make sure any dividends or interest payouts are directly reinvested to take advantage of compounding interest.

# RISK MANAGEMENT

The more financially secure you become, the more important it is to reduce the risk of losing your money or otherwise being affected by financial setbacks. The more money you have, the more you can also lose. There's not much point spending years carefully building a financial life if, in the blink of an eye, it can all be taken away from you.

Unlikely to happen, you think? How about a house fire that destroys your house and all your belongings? What if you lost your job and you could no longer make your mortgage payments? Your partner might become seriously ill, or somebody might have an accident and drive into your car or lawn, resulting in much devastation and several thousands of dollars in damage.

Unfortunately, I can go on for quite a bit longer with a list of possible accidents and scenarios that might set you back years when it comes to building a secure financial life. Let's not let that happen to you. Any of the situations above would already involve substantial emotional consequences. Suffice it to say that you wouldn't want to also worry about the financial consequences.

Luckily, you can take specific measures to allow for most risks to be covered by a security net that you weave to protect your money and your family from financial ruin. With a combination of the five most essential insurance policies, setting up or updating your will, and building a specific 3–6-months-expenses cushion, you can minimize the risk posed by most of these situations, thereby reducing the consequences of setbacks.

In this section of the *30 Days to Financial Excellence*, you'll furthermore widen your scope and think about the financial situations of others by sharing time, knowledge, or financial resources with them.

# Day 23

Risk management and insurance make up an important part of financial planning, although they are surprisingly often overlooked. Many people feel insurance policies are boring, complicated, or not needed, but years of careful financial planning amounts to nothing if a small oversight on your side leads to a financial disaster for you and your family due to an unfortunate event. That's why today you're going to take stock of your insurance policies and make sure you are adequately protected.

An insurance policy is essentially financial protection you set up against the risks of a possible loss. Choosing which types of insurance you need and which ones you do not need, and making sure the ones you have are up-to-date and applicable to your current situation, can be a bit of a challenge, though. Below are the five most common types of insurance most people need:

1. **A life insurance policy** covers others who financially rely on you and would be at risk of economic harm if you were to pass away. This might be your children, your partner, or a family member who needs ongoing care. This is also particularly relevant if you have a big debt together with somebody else, such as a mortgage or a business loan.

2.  **A health insurance policy** covers your health bills to ensure you have access to the medical care you and your family might need (or at least basic and emergency care) without afterward being presented with excessive bills to pay.

3.  **A disability insurance policy** provides you with financial compensation in the event of a disability that stops you from going back to work. It covers a certain percentage of your wages, often around 60–70%, either until you are able to go back to work again or for as long as the policy states that you are entitled to the compensation.

4.  **A homeowner or renter's insurance policy** covers you against theft or damage of your property so that if anything happened, you would get financial compensation to replace or repair what was lost.

5.  **Car insurance** often covers medical as well as property costs after a car accident for you and your passengers and even (in some cases) third parties involved.

Insurance comes in many formats and coverage types; you can usually get basic insurance which covers just a small part of any damage in limited circumstances, up to comprehensive policies that cover almost any situation or bill. Of course, the more coverage and security, the more you pay for it too.

Apart from these five most common types of insurance policies, there are many other types available, from travel to dental to pet insurance. Some might be useful to consider, while many others are probably very unlikely to be of any use to you, but that all depends on your personal situation and lifestyle. For now, let's at least make sure you have the essential five sorted.

*Day 23* **ACTION PLAN**
# Assess and adjust your insurance coverage.

1. Determine which of the five abovementioned insurance policies you logically need. Of course, if there is any other obvious kind you require due to your specific situation, add it to the list.

2. Find the policies or details for any insurance you currently have.

3. Check to make sure you have insurance for what you feel you need and consider canceling any that are no longer applicable to your situation. Confirm that all your insurance policies are still up-to-date and decide whether you need more or less coverage. Some typical situations in which you might need to update your insurance include having children, buying a house, purchasing a new vehicle, and inheriting or acquiring high-value possessions.

4. Request additional quotes from other companies to compare conditions and prices.

5. Contact your insurance company to make any changes that you decide are needed.

6. Adjust your spending plan to account for any changes you make in insurance policy payments.

7. Review your policies once a year to keep them up-to-date. Put a reminder in your calendar so you won't forget.

# Day 24

## SET UP A WILL

N ow that you've come this far in your financial organization and have begun to get a grip on your immediate and long-term needs and situation, let's make sure your money matters are well looked after even beyond that horizon. And that includes planning for your death. Not a very nice thought to entertain yourself with, but not needing to worry about your financial settlement and knowing your grieving family needn't think about how you might have wanted to pass on your money is a huge stress reliever and something you should never underestimate or leave until later.

For some, this step will not be fun, as it's not a very cheerful thought to be considering arrangements for after your death. If you feel too unmotivated or pessimistic to get started on this, know that this is totally normal and understandable. Just acknowledge your feelings and appreciate them for what they are, but don't use them as an excuse not to do this. You might never feel particularly cheerful and excited about this topic, so there is no point in saying to yourself you'll do this when you feel more like it. Just do it today and get it over with.

With each small step of today's plan you take, be grateful for how much easier it might make the grieving period for your loved ones if they don't need to work out (or fight over, as isn't uncommon) your estate. Then take an extra moment to appreciate being alive on this day and recognize that the relevance of this topic is, hopefully, still a long way away in the future.

The first thing you need to think about is a will: a ratified document that states how you would like your possessions to be divided and passed on after your demise. Bear in mind that in some countries or states the signing of a will might need to be done in the presence of a lawyer or notary in order for it to be legally valid, meaning you will need to set aside some money for this.

A second step you should take is to check whom you have named as your beneficiaries for some of your assets, such as a life insurance policy or retirement fund. If your named heirs as indicated by your will are different from the beneficiaries designated for these assets, there is a conflict of information, which might result in a court's needing to get involved to decide who will inherit that particular asset. Avoid the potential hassle by double-checking that the information is the same in both places.

## Day 24 ACTION PLAN
## Make sure your financial wishes outlive you.

1. Decide how you would like to divide your inheritance and who should inherit what. Think about your partner, children, other family members, friends, and charities.

2. Check who you have named as beneficiaries on some of your assets and whether you need to get them changed to align them with the information contained in your will.

3. Meet with a notary or estate attorney to draft your will.

4. Make it a habit to check, every few years, that your will is still up-to-date. Once again, add a reminder in your calendar.

# Day 25

## DON'T TAKE YOUR SITUATION FOR GRANTED

You've already done some great contingency planning in the last few days by setting up a will and checking your insurance policies. We'll continue to plan for adversity for one more day to close any last possible safety gaps.

Now, I am not advocating that you should prepare detailed plans on how you would deal with any possible misfortune that could happen. I would even say it's impossible to plan very extensively for them, as each one can pan out very differently to greater or lesser extents. But it won't do any harm to take a step back now and again and remember how lucky you are with the things you have (even things you might take for granted, such as having a roof over your head and food on the table every night) and to remind yourself of all the assets you've built up. And, while you're at it, remember that misfortunes could happen and that it's important to have some awareness of their consequences. Find a few minutes to do a quick review of the security nets you have in place to deal with at least some possible setbacks, and take some preventative measures to reduce your overall financial exposure.

Here are some possible scenarios that might throw you off track:

★ The loss of your job or a reduction in your contracted number of hours

★ Your partner losing their job

★ A divorce

★ A short- or long-term medical condition, be that yours, your partner's, a child's, or a parent's

★ Losing all your savings

## *Day 25* ACTION PLAN
# Appreciate and protect what you have.

1. Express gratitude. Grab a pen and write down everything that comes to mind that you are grateful for. Keep adding to it in future days or start a habit of writing down three things every evening you were particularly grateful for that day.

2. Don't take your situation for granted, and remember that all the things you have and are grateful for are also things that many others lack and long to have.

3. Take a look at the list above showing adverse situations that might come to pass and ask yourself how you would financially deal with these. (Of course, there would also be the emotional side of how you would deal with any of those, and while I don't want to disregard the emotional consequences, they unfortunately don't fit into the topic of this book.)

4. Think about steps you might need to take to have some buffer or security measures in place for some of the above situations; for instance, can you easily cut out $100 in monthly expenses if you or your partner have a sudden decrease in income? What if you had to do with $500 less a month? What changes would you need to make? How about if you lost half of your (combined) income? Can you scale up your side hustle quickly to earn a bit more money if needed? What if a family member became ill and you decided to care for them? What consequences would that have? Consider setting up a 3–6-months-expenses fund in savings that would tide you over and pay for your expenses for some time if you ever found yourself without an income.

# Day 26

## PASS IT ON

A beautiful side effect of becoming more financially savvy is the option to now share your new financial skills, either directly or indirectly, with others and help them benefit from your newly acquired level of financial excellence. Remember how privileged you are in having money to be managed in the first place and having enough to look after yourself. It's a cliché, but certainly one to not forget, that most people in the world are in a much less advantageous situation.

Let's look at how you can give back to others to help them with their financial education or worries.

### Charity

The first way to give back or pass it on is by giving to charity. This needn't cost you hundreds of dollars a year. It is just like saving money: start with it early, even if you can only contribute $1 a month or $10 a year. Not only is that still $10 a year, but it also gets you into the habit of giving, so every time you have a little more money available, it will be easy to also increase your contribution to the charity of your choice, even if it is by just a small amount. It also helps to remember that there are many who are less fortunate than you and to whom your (however small) contribution can make a considerable difference.

Apart from monthly or yearly financial contributions, or if you feel you don't currently have that space in your spending plan to donate, consider taking up a charity in your will, or giving them your time instead of money by volunteering, to help out with a fundraiser or an awareness campaign.

## Children and finances

Whether you have children of your own, grandchildren, or (adopted) nieces and nephews, or plan to have children at some point in the future, you can play an important role in educating them financially as another way to pass on your financial development. Some ideas include:

★ Give children a small amount of pocket money from an early age to get them to plan how they want to spend it and how to save up for a bigger purchase. It teaches them the value of saving, planning, and prioritizing.

★ Consider some type of savings match or interest you give children for every dollar they save if they do not yet have a savings account with a bank.

★ Give each child three jars: one for spending money that they can always use, one for savings that they assign to a specific savings objective, and one for donating to a charity of their choice.

★ Have a chores list with tasks they can do in and around the house to earn some extra money. You can set a maximum amount per week or month they can earn if you want to limit how much to pay them. In this way, they learn how they can earn money and how this can help speed up a savings goal.

★ Teach children about debt and its financial implications in the long run. The best way for them to learn this is by giving them a small loan for a purchase they would like to make and charging interest on it until they pay off their loan with you. A tough but no doubt very valuable lesson.

## Set aside money for your children

Another way to help others financially is by setting aside some money in a savings or investment account, for example, for your children or grandchildren.

Not only will this give you a great way, once they are a little older, to show them the power of compound interest, it also makes for an unmatchable eighteenth or twenty-first birthday present, or a wedding gift.

The earlier you do this, the more time the money has to grow. If you are lucky enough to live in a country that has a child benefit scheme, in which parents or guardians of children receive a regular social security payment to help pay for the cost of children, you can even consider setting some of this aside. If you were able to invest $75 per month from your child's or grandchild's birth, this would grow to a total of more than $32,700 by the time your beneficiary is eighteen years old, assuming an average return rate of 7%.

Of course, you might not be able to set this much aside. If that's the case, don't automatically assume you can't invest any money. Consider saving half of it, or just $25 or $10 a month if that's more doable for you. Even $10 set aside each month will grow to $4,365 after 18 years, still a very worthy sum to anybody at that age!

# *Day 26* ACTION PLAN
## Enjoy planning the gift of giving.

1. Think about how you could contribute time or money to a charity on a regular or just a one-off basis. Decide on the type of charity you'd like to fund, and if you can make a monetary contribution, make sure to allow for it in your spending plan too.

2. If you have any children, grandchildren, nieces, or nephews, consider how you can pass on some of your financial knowledge to them in an age-appropriate way.

3. Decide if you want to set up a savings or investment fund for your (grand)children with a regular monthly contribution. If so, make sure to open a different account for each and update your spending plan if needed. Check carefully for the conditions as you might not be able to put a minor as the beneficiary of an account, meaning you'd have to include it in your will to make sure it goes to them if you passed away before they reach adulthood.

# YOUR FINANCIAL FUTURE

In the last few weeks, you've done a lot of hard work, put in time and effort to improve your finances, and started off on the path to financial excellence. Of course, you don't want all that energy to have been spent in vain. Financial excellence doesn't stop when you reach day 30. It is a continuous process, made up of many of the habits you've started on this journey, a change in attitude, and repeatedly taking small steps that guide you off the path to a financially average life that you had until you began this program. The small advances you make each time will slowly but steadily get you to the alternative: the road to financial excellence.

Once you're on that new path, however, it is easy to stray back to your old path—the one that felt more comfortable, was easier, and along which many other people were pushing you, not by choice, but because you all happened to be following the crowd and doing what everybody else does. There, you didn't need to think; you could carry consumer debt because everybody does. You didn't need to plan ahead for your retirement—nobody does, and surely it will be okay. The others around you showed up with a new car, fancy gadget, or photos from their last faraway holiday, so you'd run off and help yourself to one of those too.

Your new path is much less trodden. In fact, it's much harder going at first. There aren't many people pushing you ahead. And there are a lot more obstacles on the road you have to overcome all by yourself—things you don't know about or that none of your friends do. You can hear people in the distance shouting at you to come back, to not be silly, or they laugh at you as you wander off in a direction that's less familiar and less comfortable.

But you know what? That's okay. If you just follow what everybody else is doing, you'll just end up like everybody else: with financial stress, a big debt, vulnerability to your boss's whims and management style—which, even if you don't like it, you have to put up with as you need the money to afford your lifestyle—an insecure retirement plan (or no retirement plan at all), and no emergency measures in place for when you face a setback and you need to fall back upon other ways of financing your life.

Trust me when I say there are three ways you'll be enormously grateful you took this second path:

- ★ **It will become more motivating the longer you stay on it.** Once you start seeing the effects of the new steps you're taking (your debt going down, an emergency fund accruing, your savings going up, more income), you'll gain momentum and feel more comfortable and convinced you've taken the right path.

★ **It will become easier.** By making decisions now, you no longer need to make them every month. Decision stress is a real thing and often leads to inaction. As you are building strong financial habits you will benefit from these actions for the rest of your life. You'll learn more as you go along, meaning you can ignore the seductive calls from the people over on the other path more easily. You might even be able to help one or two of them find their way to the new path too.

★ **You'll be able to live out your dreams.** Your financial life will become more and more secure, you'll make more money through your side hustle, and you can save up for your various goals. You won't need to go and live on the street or back with your parents if you lose your job. You'll be able to retire with enough funds.

So while it was much harder at first, it will become much easier later on. The further along you get, the more difficult the *other* path becomes: people start to struggle to pay back their debts, and even more so if they lose their jobs. When they get to retirement age and would like to take a step back to enjoy their time, they need to work harder than ever not to lose their jobs to a younger generation. The further down the line you go, the more obvious it will become you took the right path. But don't expect them to admit this! They'd much rather blame others, life events, or society for their problems—and not their own inaction.

But, of course, you're only at the beginning and you've only just set off on the path to financial excellence. The path to financial ordinariness is still very close and attractive. In fact, you can, even now, hear it calling you to come back.

So how do you make sure not to slide back and end up with the rest? Let's finish off this 30-day plan with some very easy ways to make sure you don't wander back into mediocrity. Let's make it as easy as possible for you to stay on the path to financial excellence.

# Day 27

## VISUALIZE, TRACK, AND CELEBRATE YOUR VICTORIES

Reaching financial excellence is an exciting but also a long process you need to keep up with over time. No matter how motivated you are to get your financial life in order and invest in your financial future, there will be times when that motivation fails you, when it seems too much work, and when you want to give in to the instant desires and distractions around you instead of working out how to deal with your money responsibly.

Here are three techniques you can use to combat those feelings or temptations and stick with your plan:

### Visualize

Start by visualizing what you are working toward. Close your eyes for a moment and picture your financial life being organized: you know where your money is going, you have a savings account that is growing each month, and you know the different goals you are saving up for and how much you need for each one. Your retirement plan is on track and you've set yourself clear income goals that you are pursuing via a new income stream. Your debt is no longer growing; in fact, you are slowly crushing the debts you still have, and you have a target date for when you'll be completely debt-free.

Feel the peace knowing all these areas are under control or that at least you are going in the right direction and making progress on all these fronts. Compare this with the stress, insecurity, anxiety, and dejection you might have felt in the past when thinking about your finances and future. Appreciate the feeling of reassurance that you are actively managing your money now, and that you have grown to be confident about your personal finances.

## Track

When setting yourself new goals, make it a habit to also start tracking your progress toward each goal in a fun, visual, creative way. This can be as simple as a page with 100 squares, each worth $100 to represent the $10,000 you're paying off in debts in your diary, a paper on your fridge, or on chalkboard painted on the inside of your wardrobe. By making your goal visible, it instantly becomes real, and when you update your progress toward your goal regularly, you will feel the instant gratification and feedback of seeing how you've moved closer to your goal. For fun and creative ideas, check out Pinterest or other social media where you can find myriad beautiful and simple financial goal trackers.

## Celebrate

Here's something many people forget on their way to reaching goals: celebrate! Not only the end goal, but celebrate the smaller steps too. Rome wasn't built in a day, and you won't save $20,000 or pay off your debts overnight either. Break down your goals into smaller milestones, and then when you reach them, treat yourself to something. This can be anything that makes you feel celebratory: a night out to the movies, a coffee out with your best friend, a visit to a spa, or whatever it is that makes you feel happy and gives you a pat on the back for how much you've achieved already. (Although you want to be mindful that it doesn't cost lots of money, as that would set you behind on your plan again.)

*Day 27* **ACTION PLAN**
# Identify and celebrate your successes.

1. Create a vision board with pictures or quotes of what you are aiming for with your new financial you: becoming debt-free and attaining peace of mind, your retirement goals, or maybe a new secondhand car paid completely up front. Put your board or collage in a prominent place and look at it with full attention, at least every morning or evening, to remind yourself of your objectives.

2. Determine your main financial goals for the next few months and start tracking your progress on each one. Write the end goal at the top of each financial tracker, then every time you get a little closer to that goal, update your progress.

3. Set smaller milestones for each of your goals. For each milestone, decide what you will be doing to celebrate. Write that along with each milestone on your tracker. The prospect of the treat you have in store for yourself might motivate you to reach your goal even faster!

# Day 28

## SORT YOUR PAPERWORK

An exceptional financial life goes hand in hand with a well-set-up home office. This requires a clean and inviting workspace to pay bills, update your spending plan, and otherwise work on your finances, a space in which important documents are filed away regularly and can be located quickly when needed.

Let's have a closer look at the three essentials to having an organized financial system.

The first things you'll need are some folders or files where you can keep your documents. Each folder should have a topic, for example, "house," "car," "medical," etc. These can be further divided into categories. In "house," you might have "mortgage," "electric bills," and "property tax," to name just a few. Use dividers to separate the different categories. Keep your documents in reverse chronological order: oldest ones at the back, newest ones at the front.

If you want to minimize the amount of paperwork in your house, consider going paperless and keeping all your files in digital format. You'll probably need to invest in a small scanner so you can scan any paperwork you don't also have a digital copy of. You'll want to file all your documents in a logical and easily accessible digital way, so make sure to set up a similar folder structure on your computer as described above and to keep backups saved somewhere physically, such as a backup hard drive, or in the cloud.

Second, you need a workstation or home office somewhere in your house that is a pleasant place to be with enough lighting, a regulated temperature, a good chair, and maybe some inviting objects such as a family photo or a plant to liven things up. Have your most-used stationery and supplies at hand, such as pens, a stapler and staples, envelopes, a hole puncher, and a scanner, if applicable. Have your folders with your paperwork handy. This is where you'll process your documents, pay bills, and plan your spending and financial goals. The easier and more comfortable this place is, the more likely you'll want to spend time there working on your financial life.

Last, I recommend you set up a mail-sorting station right next to your front door. Put up four baskets or folders to divide the mail you receive as soon as you open it: to file, to read, to do, and to recycle.

Once a week, take the "to read" and "to do" baskets to your home office and process each document, then put it in the "to file" or "to recycle" basket. Once a month, put away all documents in the "to recycle" bin as well as the "to file" bin.

# *Day 28* ACTION PLAN
## Create a home office that sets you up to succeed.

1. Set up or review your filing system. Create adequate and relevant categories for your household, either with physical files or online with digital ones.

2. Do a quick route through your home and gather all paperwork that can be processed, filed, or recycled.

3. Create a pleasant workspace in which to work on your finances, and have your paperwork or filing systems handy.

4. Set up a mail station or control center next to your front door from which you can instantly deal with any incoming mail. Open and sort your mail into the correct baskets daily, read and process it once a week, and file or shred and recycle everything on a set day each month.

# Day 29

## MAKE A LONG-TERM PLAN

As we're getting to the end of this 30-day plan and looking toward the future at what's beyond, now is the perfect time to gain clarity on where you want your life to go and, in particular, how you would like to see your financial situation develop. Your hard work in the last few weeks on the various tasks will allow you to put it all together and make a long-term roadmap and plan for your finances—the more specific, the better.

You can use your notes, plans, and the action plans from the previous days to go through all the topics we've looked at and start setting targets for each one on various timescales: start with your savings and decide how much you would like to have in savings in one year's time. What about in three years, five years, etc.?

Do the same for your debt, income, retirement funds, and personal investments. Here are some timelines that are good short-, mid-, and long-term moments in the future.

- ★ 1 year
- ★ 3 years
- ★ 5 years
- ★ 10 years
- ★ 25 years

Of course, more money isn't going to appear in one year just because you once wrote it down. In order for your dreams to come true, you need to know how you're going to achieve them: you need a plan, and then you need to work that plan. For each area and timeline, note down what you need to do to reach your targets.

Say your plan is to have $3,000 extra in savings by the end of the year; then you need to be clear that this represents an extra $250 for each of the next twelve months. Study your spending plan and determine where that money is going to come from every single month from now on. Which expenses are you cutting out, or how are you increasing your income? Once you have your situation in a year's time mapped out, plan for three, then five, ten, and twenty-five years in the future.

Get into the habit of reviewing your plan once a year—around New Year's, during tax season, or at the start of the new academic year are usually good moments. Check how you are doing compared to one year ago. Update your targets or create new ones and keep an active plan to achieve those goals.

## $\mathcal{D}ay$ 29 ACTION PLAN
## Set your long-term goals.

1. Set specific goals for each of the financial areas for one, three, five, ten and twenty-five years. Don't overcomplicate, but feel free to adapt these years if that makes more sense to you. Do this for debts, savings, income, retirement funds, and investments and add others if you want to. You might want to set a target for your net worth, mindset, or expenses too, for example.

2. Looking at your one- and three-year plans to start with, how do you aim to achieve those goals? Which adjustments do you need to make in your spending and income potential to reach those goals? Write down specific tactics you will employ to achieve your targets.

3. Have a set moment each year to review your goals, and then adjust your plan accordingly. Mark this appointment with yourself in your calendar.

# Day 30

## MONEY MISTAKES TO AVOID

As we're now on the very last day of this 30-day course, and after having looked at all the things to do to start moving toward financial excellence, I'd like to finish off with some tips on what to avoid or, indeed, what *not* to do:

### Not living below your means

A new computer, designer clothes, or that bigger house you lay your eyes on can all be tempting you continuously to spend more money. Make it your principal objective to always live below your means, and ask yourself whether you really need the next thing you're about to purchase. Spend less than you earn and save or invest the money left over to build a financially stable future. Don't buy things on credit that you don't need that might put you in financial difficulty or that aren't within your budget. If you live above your means, you can't also be financially secure. Don't try to keep up with the Joneses, buying new or bigger things just because that is what they are doing. Follow your own plan and priorities.

### Giving in to lifestyle inflation

Linked to the previous point is the trap we all fall into with time: lifestyle inflation, or the slow but steady devaluation of our lifestyle and our rising expectations. What we first thought to be a great part of our life (a low-budget-hotel stay, our new mobile phone) with time loses its value and comes to seem below our worth. This makes us always want more, bigger, and better with time. Be aware of this, make an effort to appreciate what you have, and don't give in to the feeling of something being beneath your station. If your car, mobile phone, or laptop is still perfectly safe and doing what it should be doing, then hold off replacing it until this is really needed. You were once excited to own it, so bring back that feeling and get more out of it.

## Being unaware of the impact of fees

Don't underestimate the impact of fees and interest rates over long periods of time. Take a moment today to calculate the total amount of interest you will end up paying on your mortgage or another long-term loan you have. If you invest money or are thinking of starting to invest at some point soon, look carefully at the fees you might be charged: maintenance, research fees, load fees, and trading fees are just a few examples. A fee might seem small now, but over time it can have enormous consequences for your finances. A thousand dollars invested yearly with a 7% return will grow to more than $96,000 in thirty years' time at a yearly 0.25% fee (low-cost index investing), but only to just over $68,000 in a 2% account (think mutual funds).

## Not countering inflation

A healthy economy has a yearly inflation rate of about 2–3%. That means that each year, money loses about that percentage in value. What once cost $100 will cost $102 the year after, $104 in two years' time, $122 in ten years, and $164 in twenty-five years at a 2% inflation rate; with 3%, the price would be $209 after twenty-five years. When you calculate your needs for retirement, which is often many years in the future, make sure to correct for inflation. If you think you need $1,500 a month for when you are retired, remember this will need to be approximately $2,460 in twenty-five years with a 2% inflation rate, or $3,140 at 3% inflation. Adjust your numbers each year, and make sure to close the gap between the current and future value of your money. An easy way to keep up is to always increase your yearly contributions to your savings or retirement accounts just above the inflation rate; for example, if you contribute $100 a month this year, make sure to increase this to $103 next year.

## Not scheduling time regularly to maintain your financial organization/life

One of the most important things—if not *the* most important thing—you can do to improve your financial life is to schedule in time regularly to keep up with your finances. Without regular check-in moments when you dedicate some focused time, it is hard to stay on top of this area, and it will indeed be hard to make sure that all the progress you've made over the past few weeks isn't going to go to waste. If you don't know where to start, in the appendix, I give an overview of how often to check in with each financial area or habit.

# $\mathcal{D}ay$ 30 ACTION PLAN
## Trim the fat that costs you money.

1. Have a critical look at some purchases you are planning to make in the short term and determine whether these are really needed and fit in with your spending plan. Do you need to spend that money, or are you able to hold on with what you have for a little longer? Are you wanting these things more than you need them because of social pressure or a particular image they portray? Could you use the money in a better way for now?

2. Check any investment and bank accounts for hidden fees such as maintenance fees, card fees, and others. See if you can negotiate these fees or whether it is worth changing banks.

3. Set a day in your calendar to review your yearly contributions to your savings, investments and retirement accounts. Add a reminder to top them up with at least the inflation rate from the previous year as well as 50% of any salary increases you've had.

4. Schedule in regular time to work on your finances. Develop daily, weekly, and monthly habits to stay on top of your money, and keep progressing on the path that you started 30 days ago. Your future self will be grateful!

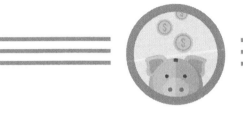

# WHAT'S NEXT

Well done for making it to the end of this journey to your new financial self! In the past 30 days, you have created order in the chaos that was once your financial life. You've implemented good money habits, begun your journey to becoming debt-free, started investing in a secure and richer financial future, and set yourself goals to keep progressing on the path to financial excellence. I truly hope that by now you feel there is structure in your personal finances, and that even if it hasn't all translated into everything being exactly where you want it to be, at least you feel you are on the right track, that you have clearer in your mind what you are working toward, and that you know how to go on from here. Most importantly, I hope your new financial life has translated into an increase in your happiness.

Of course, you're not there yet, and I bet there will be days when it's all a bit much and things don't go as planned. You know what? That's totally fine, as that's what it feels like at times to me too.

But hey, you've started, and that is the most important thing you can do. You've begun to change your financial disorganization, stress, and feelings of scarcity into a life of financial organization and excellence, free of worries, and with a feeling of abundance.

And all of that in just 30 days—that's a pretty awesome change, if you ask me. From here on, I encourage you to keep up the work to continue down the path you've taken and achieve ever greater changes by using the power of compound interest, freeing up more and more money from paying off your debts, and generating extra income from a side hustle. Make sure to check the appendix to review how to stay on top of the various elements you've implemented. Here's to a new financial you—the new personal finance ninja!

# Appendix

## ACTION STEPS: MAKE YOUR PRECIOUS TIME COUNT

| Frequency | Task | Day | Time | Total Time |
|-----------|------|-----|------|------------|
| Daily | Sort through incoming paperwork | 28 | 2 minutes | 10 minutes |
| | Read your affirmations from day 2. Move on to a new level if any of the affirmations are no longer uncomfortable. | 2 | 3 minutes | |
| | Track your spending | 3 | 5 minutes | |
| Weekly | Work out how much you've saved from cutting out an expense | 4 | 3 minutes | 15–20 minutes plus 1–10 hours on your side hustle |
| | Process bills and other paperwork | 28 | 15 minutes | |
| | Work on your side hustle | 16 | 1–10 hours | |

| | | | | |
|---|---|---|---|---|
| Monthly | Calculate your savings rate from the previous month | 8 | 5 minutes | 1–1.5 hours |
| | Update your goal trackers | 27 | 5 minutes | |
| | Calculate your new net worth | 10 | 10 minutes | |
| | Update your monthly income and income goals | 15 and 17 | 10 minutes | |
| | File your paperwork | 28 | 10 minutes | |
| | Create a new spending plan for next month | 5 | 15 minutes | |
| | Update your outstanding debts and paying-off plans | 12 and 13 | 15 minutes | |
| Quarterly or Yearly | Make sure your emergency fund still has enough in it | 14 | 2 minutes | 2–2.5 hours plus 1–20 hours on your personal capital |
| | Check how much you have in your retirement funds | 19 | 5 minutes | |
| | Increase your contributions to your retirement funds | 21 | 10 minutes | |
| | Check that your will is up to date | 24 | 15 minutes | |
| | Check in with and update all your savings goals | 7 | 20 minutes | |
| | Audit your insurance | 23 | 20 minutes | |
| | Update your long-term financial plans | 29 | 1 hour | |
| | Invest in your personal capital | 18 | 1–20 hours | |

# A small request

## Enjoyed this book? You can make a big difference!

I hope this book has shown you how to reach financial excellence and establish healthy financial habits.

Reviews are one of the most powerful tools to get more readers to find my book. As an author with a small following, it's a long process to get the word out and get the online stores' algorithms to boost visibility of this book. A review not only helps others know you recommend this book, it also helps visibility, as the more reviews, the higher the likelihood online shops will show my books when readers are searching for new books to read.

If you enjoyed this book and found it helpful, I'd be really grateful if you could spend just a few minutes writing a review.

Thank you very much!
Inge

# Acknowledgments

Thank you to my editors, Chris Noel, Susannah Noel, and Sheryl Rapée-Adams, for their brilliant contributions and suggestions.

Heidi Dorr was once again amazing proofreading this book.

Domini Dragoone has, like last time, outdone herself with the cover and interior design, and I'm grateful for her suggestions along the way.

EbookPbook has once again done a fantastic job maintaining this book's beautiful design in digital format.

My sister, Martine Hol, continues to motivate me to pursue my dreams and to do what I love today instead of leaving it until tomorrow.

A special thank you to my husband, Douglas Haines, for his encouragement and patience throughout the process and his never-wavering support.

# About the Author

Inge Natalie Hol is an author, personal finance coach, and educator and runs two businesses. She is passionate about helping others improve their financial lives and start living out their dreams.

She lives with her husband, two rescue cats, and three rescue dogs in Spain.

Inge Natalie Hol also wrote *100 Steps to Financial Independence: The Definitive Roadmap to Achieving Your Financial Dreams*.

Inge also runs a weekly podcast, *The Financial Harmoney Podcast*, which is available on all major podcast platforms.

You can connect with Inge via her website www.ingenataliehol.com and:

Twitter (twitter.com/ingenataliehol)
Facebook (facebook.com/ingenataliehol)
Instagram (instagram.com/ingenataliehol)
IngeNatalieHol.com/books

More books coming soon.

Printed by Amazon Italia Logistica S.r.l.
Torrazza Piemonte (TO), Italy

28115290R00076